The Link is What You Think

and may we share simcha, love, nachas and growth for many years to come in good health as a team, and in abundance.

Remember - we open the eye of the needle - H" creates miracles. They are right there in front of us. Let's merit to see them.

with much love, admiration & gratitude

Sarah Etel

The Link is What You Think

Michael R. Mantell, Ph.D.

ISBN-13: 9781977670496
ISBN-10: 1977670490

More Powerful Praise for Dr. Mantell's
The Link is What You Think

Dr. Mantell is one of the most thoughtful and clear communicators I have ever had the pleasure of working with. No matter how big or small the project is he comes with the same amount of passion and brain-power. I would not be where I am today without his support and his perspective on many issues. Simply, he can help any company in any department on any project or role!
MICHAEL PIERMONT
VICE-PRESIDENT OF SALES AND OPERATIONS AT FOODA

Dr. Mantell has done it again! What I love about Michael's book is that he distills tactics and habits that will help you grow, succeed and become your very best. This is a book with "daily doses" of inspiration to share with colleagues, friends, and family. I highly recommend reading this great book filled with life transforming, powerful thoughts and advice.
BRYAN K. O'ROURKE, MBA
INVESTOR, SPEAKER AND BUSINESS ADVISOR,
CEO FITNESS INDUSTRY TECHNOLOGY
COUNCIL, FOUNDER VEDERE VENTURES

"Dr. Mantell's latest book is filled with wisdom and insights that will positively help you change the way you think and feel. As Founder and CEO of Wellness Educators (WE) I've relied on Dr. Mantell's impressive behavior change expertise to craft our wellness programs to benefit our referring physicians, our world-class health and wellness coaches, and our clients coast to coast. This is a

must read book for anyone seeking positive changes to their mindset to live a more balanced life."
GARY GURIAN, MTP, BCS
FOUNDER/CEO, WE WELLNESS EDUCATORS

"Michael Mantell is able to communicate deep and ancient wisdom in the most simple and easy to implement way. His ideas and insights are timeless and are guaranteed to upgrade the lives of those fortunate enough to be exposed to them."
ETHAN PENNER
FINANCIAL MARKET PIONEER, PROFESSOR, ECONOMIC PHILOSOPHER, FITNESS ENTREPRENEUR

Miracles! That's what will occur in your life, and subsequently the lives of others, by applying Dr. Mantell's easy to understand principles. Game changer! In a profound and endearing, yet down to earth, way. Masterpiece!
ALLISON ROSS
AUTHOR AND FORMER TELEVISION NEWS ANCHOR FOR NBC-TV AND CBS-TV IN SAN DIEGO, NEWZY AT KPHO PHOENIX & KVOA TUCSON

"The pathway to success is helped by a daily prescription of a better way to think and live. The only drug needed here is Dr. Mantell's written word on your journey to an enriching and full life. This is an "extra copy book" that's meant for you to share with those who have special meaning in your life."
LEONARD C. WRIGHT, CPA/PFS, CGMA, CFP, CLU, ChFC
FORMER HOST OF "FINANCIAL FRIDAYS" RADIO SHOW & "MONEY DOCTOR" FOR THE AMERICAN INSTITUTE OF CPAs

Dr. Mantell may have saved the best for last, this book is a must have for anyone truly seeking self-improvement! His time-honored insights are among our clients' favorites at PFC Fitness Camp where amazing people come from all over the world seeking optimal health... I can't wait to send them home with this tool!
ZACH CUTLER
Managing Partner, Premier Fitness Camp, Omni La Costa Resort and Spa

No matter what the issue, from family to friends to careers, 'The Daily 5' illuminates a solution to worries and problems everyday for me. The "sun will come out tomorrow" may be the song, but with 'The Daily 5', the sun comes up when you read the day's Mantell mantra.
NANETTE WISER
WRITER, EDITOR, BLOGGER, CONTENT PRODUCER
WEBSITES, SOCIAL MEDIA, SEO
COMMUNICATIONS, PUBLIC RELATIONS & MARKETING

Acknowledgments

Mark Twain observed, "*To get the full value of joy you must have someone to divide it with.*" How blessed and fortunate I am to live this simple wisdom to the fullest with purpose, passion and a genuine sense of privilege in my pursuit of helping clients around the world.

This book has taken nearly 69 years to write. I've been most fortunate to learn the wisdom that fill these pages from loving, supportive, parents and grandparents. My clients, as well, teach me a great deal.

"*Michael, what do you care what they think?*" my mother would daily teach me. "*Michael, stop talking it into yourself,* " my grandmother would daily teach me. Grateful? Pfff. "*Michael, of course we're going to work today…we love what we do,*" my Dad would say to me from the time I was seven years old working in one of his stores. Thankful, appreciative, indebted, beholden, much obliged -- just begin to scratch the surface of my feelings.

Since the day she stepped on the back of my shoe walking down the hall of West Orange Mountain High School on January 26, 1966, and I turned and looked at Paula for the first time, immediately telling my friend, "Someday I'm going to marry her," my life was made better. We married on December 19, 1971 and ever since we've given definition to "*happily ever after.*" At each other's side every step of the way, through good times and harder times, this book belongs to her.

After all, she encouraged me to write each book I have, and Paula is fully credited for creating the phrase, *"The Link is What You Think."*

I want to thank my brother, Dr. Gary, for helping create the overall look and feel of the book. I also want to thank Nanette Wiser for suggesting, "Mantell's Daily 5" and for asking me to serve as Health & Wellness Curator for St. Pete Life Magazine. I have special thanks to our friends Drs. Anne and Howard Winter, with whom we enjoy sharing so much of life. Of course, I am particularly grateful to Teaneck, NJ Councilman, Mark J. Schwartz, for so kindly linking me to Mayor Mohammed Hameeduddin, who wrote a very gracious forward to this book.

The love of our children, Ben and Jonathan, Ben's wife and our wonderful daughter-in-law Kristin, our six grandchildren Judah, Kayla, Eli, Rebecca, Jacob and Max have sustained us. We've been blessed in so many ways, beyond description, though our children and grandchildren certainly are at the top of the list. This book and the ideas I've shared here for a better life, are my gift to them.

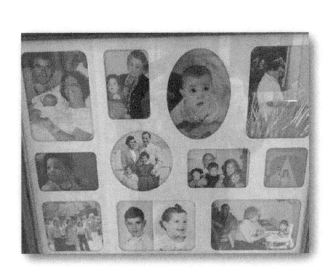

Forward

Mayor Mohammed Hameeduddin
Teaneck, New Jersey

Imagine disagreeing with others respectfully, moving past our own preconceptions and limiting beliefs to fully hear others, and proudly claim our distinct uniqueness in ways that leaves no one degraded in the process? That's just what Dr. Michael Mantell's profound, very timely and practical book wisely and practically equips us all to do.

According to the latest edition of "Civility in America" more than half of Americans expect civility to worsen over the next few years and 75% of our citizens agree that incivility has risen to crisis levels. It's time we learn to treat ourselves, and others, in healthier more civil ways that promote and advance greater personal freedom, success, happiness and wellbeing.

With a frustrating economy, challenges throughout our educational and health care systems, the ease of sharing vitriol through social media, increasing family stress and instability, a declining standard of living for so many, the media stirring our anger, the erroneous belief that one "MUST" have what one "DEMANDS," the unhealthy thought that it's "HORRIBLE, TERRIBLE AND AWFUL" when life doesn't go the way one expects or insists, and our lives filled with conflict, antagonism, quarrel, struggle, competition, raging disagreement and opposition, it's time to learn the lesson of how to free oneself of strife and negativity by understanding and applying the positive psychology woven into Dr. Mantell's, *"The Link is What You Think."* His plain speaking and straightforward skill in teaching how to elevate us from the rut of our own negative thinking, is unsurpassed.

I've followed Michael's *"Daily 5"* in social media for quite some time and am convinced that his best-in-class, time-proven tactics that he's carefully curated over decades, masterfully show us how to sow our seeds of greatness, go to higher and more successful levels in life and turn every situation we face into one where we win or learn...but never lose. For anyone who once and for all wants to crush self-imposed obstacles that keep us from being our best, this is unmatched reading.

Permeating each page of this book is Michael's experienced eye helping the reader develop a more peaceful and kind approach to him/herself and others. Dr. Mantell's "people building" success, honed over 40 years of practice, is evident throughout this much-needed, deep and yet easy to apply daily guide to an elevated life, rich with specific instruction on how to be our best selves, and live our full destiny.

In dealing with everyday life as the Mayor of a successfully diverse city such as Teaneck N.J., filled with passion and purpose to uplift the lives of my constituents as I am, I'm certain that helping others live with unconditional self-acceptance, increasing gratitude and mindfulness, banished self- and other- critical thinking, will surely lead to what we all wish for – living better lives, healthy and happy.

That's what Dr. Mantell's book will help us all do...it surely will become a *"coach in the pocket"* for many. By reading a daily dose of his wise "Daily 5" and applying his insights consistently, I'm confident you'll enjoy living a better life, healthier and with greater peace of mind.

Introduction

The other morning at my gym I overheard a man in his 40s say, "I don't think I can do that exercise, I'm afraid I'll get hurt." It's been said, "Doubt kills more dreams than failure ever has." The gym discussion is living proof of that observation. He doubted his ability to do a simple exercise because he imagined that he'd get hurt, turned away and didn't' try. I wanted to tell him, "Your arms, legs and back aren't giving out. Your mind is giving up. *The link is what you think.*"

Our bodies, indeed our entire lives, react to the way we think, which creates the way we feel and that leads to the way we behave. Stress is a great example. Look at what thinking about an event in a way that predicts gloom and doom, anticipating awful, terrible and horrible outcomes can do to your blood pressure or the lining of your stomach creating indigestion or an ulcer.

Calvin Coolidge noted, "*Don't expect to build up the weak by pulling down the strong.*" Sadly, there are so many who think, incorrectly, that life is like a see-saw. The only way they go up they incorrectly think, is to insure that they cause others to go down. Wise folks think differently and therefore don't suffer from the "*compare and despair*" syndrome – they don't see life as a win or lose, up or down proposition, but rather as one in which they always learn. They think, like all varsity thinkers do, that every setback in life is simply a set up for a very strong comeback.

"Mrs. Mantell, Michael is not college material," said my 8th grade teacher, Mrs. McCaffery at Chancellor Avenue Elementary School in 1962 to my mother in a parent-teacher conference. The two words my mom had in reply are best left unprinted. So it was no surprise when I graduated with a Ph.D. from the University of Pennsylvania, almost immediately after receiving the diploma, my mother motioned from the audience that she wanted to leave.

"But mom, I just graduated, and I thought we were all going to attend the party," I said to her and the family that were in attendance.

"No, we can celebrate later, but first let's go to the cemetery," she said. *"WHATT? The cemetery??? Why?"* I incredulously asked.

She said, *"I thought we'd visit a certain 8th grade teacher you had and show her your Penn diploma. You see, Michael, don't believe everything they tell you about you and surely don't believe everything you think,"* she wisely taught at that high point in my life. She went on to teach, *"Remember who defines you in life. You do. Not your 8th grade teacher, not your boss, not your neighbor, not anyone. Just you. So, Michael, how will you define you? What will you think about you?"*

I was challenged to apply this thinking in 1996, a number of years after my 1988, "Don't Sweat the Small Stuff PS: It's All Small Stuff" was released. That book, my first, went into three printings, had a successful audio version, was celebrated and awarded wonderful titles like "Good Morning America's" *"Hot Pick"* and "Publishers Weekly Magazine's" *"Listen Up Award: Best Audio of 1996."* Little did I ever expect any controversy from all this. What controversy?

William Safire noted in an article in the New York times, *"The Lives They Lived: 01-07-01: On Language; Stuff,"* and in his 2004 book, *"The Right Word in the Right Place at the Right Time,"* that I first popularized the expression, *"Don't Sweat the Small Stuff"* in the title of my 1988 book. But that didn't stop someone else from coming along and writing another book in 1996 using the same expression in the title of his later book.

No, *"Hey Dr. Mantell, love the title of your book, and I was wondering if you'd mind if I used it for mine if I change the "PS" to 'And.'"* No phone call, no letter, no nothing.

Here's what happened. One day in 1996, I was walking through Fashion Valley shopping mall in San Diego, and passed a Barnes and Noble bookstore. I almost fell off my feet when I gazed in the window and saw a floor to ceiling display of my book, *"Don't Sweat the Small Stuff: PS It's All Small Stuff."* Honestly, I was beaming.

After all, a young kid from Newark, NJ who went from a 1.8 GPA in my first semester of college to a Ph.D. from the University of Pennsylvania and now living in San Diego, California, seeing my first book, that I thought was out of print, so prominently displayed in Barnes and Noble...well, an immediate phone call to my wife, Paula, was in order.

"Oh my goodness! You won't believe this," I shouted in the phone to Paula. *"The book is all over Barnes and Noble."*

"Wow, that's incredible! How come we didn't know this was going to happen?" Paula wondered. I did too.

Then it hit me. *"Wait a second, that's not the cover of my book. They must have changed it,"* I told Paula. *"Hold on, something is really weird,"* I remember mumbling.

"My book was, 'PS It's All Small Stuff' not, *'AND It's All Small Stuff?!'"* Then it hit me.

"You aren't going to believe this, better sit down. Someone else used the phrase, 'Don't Sweat the Small Stuff' from my book." The very expression, I might add, that William Safire later acknowledged that I first popularized as a book title.

What followed was a long string of phone calls from family and friends, colleagues, lawyers and publishers, media and newspapers. But thanks to William Safire, he clarified the story.

"What are you going to do to that guy?" *"Did you see him in the UK's newspaper lying in the hammock with dollar bills strewn all over him?"*

I wasn't going to do anything to him. I did see the picture of him lying in a hammock covered with money all over him from head to toe. That was enough.

Sweat it? Are you kidding? I loved it. You see, things don't happen *TO* us, but rather, things happen *FOR* us! What an opportunity this was! But only because *the link is what you think.*

Like Alfred E. Neuman, the fictitious cover boy of my favorite magazine growing up, *"Mad Magazine"* who wondered, starting in the magazine's 24th issue, *"What, me Worry?"* I don't worry. I don't sweat it. Never have. Never will. It's like drinking poison and hoping the other guy suffers. Why cause suffering in myself? It's bad enough something I'd prefer not happen, actually happened. On top of that I should create suffering within myself as well. Never. Ever.

"Dr. Mantell, you wrote 'Don't Sweat the Small Stuff'?" Yes sir, I did.

"Dr. Mantell, would you come on and talk about your bestselling book, 'Don't Sweat the Small Stuff'?" Sure I would! And did. And still do.

"Dr. Mantell, I loved your book." *"Thanks, did you love mine or the other one?"* *"What other one? Wow, he stole your title!"* No, he actually didn't steal the title.

Wherever I spoke, the confusion and controversy caused by the other author was a topic to discuss and use as an example of never, ever sweating the small stuff. Never. Ever. I don't sweat it, I don't regret it, I move on and I forget it.

This current book will teach you exactly how to do the very same, and always come out feeling great about yourself. Unconditional self-acceptance is the key. You'll learn how to win or learn, but never lose.

What's my secret to not ever causing stress within myself, and especially over the shenanigans of others?

Here it is, so repeat after me: *the link is what you think.* I'll say it again: *the link is what you think.* Repeat after me: *the link is what you think.* Write it down, cut it out, paste it on the dashboard of your car or keep it on your desk, and look at it the next time you are in traffic, have a run-in with your boss, look at your bank account (if you have one), weigh yourself, or wake up in the morning and wonder what the heck you did the night before. *The link is what you think*, it's not—NOT *EVER*—the external event.

You actually think that someone else's behavior *MAKES* you upset? You believe that seeing another book by a confusingly all too similar title is worth sweating? You'd be wrong, erroneous, inaccurate, and wasting precious time in life if you answer, "yes" to these questions. Never, ever, sweat the small stuff. There's too much health and happiness to focus on. Why look at the thorns on the rose bush when you can look at the roses on the thorn bush?

After the privilege of studying with Albert Ellis, Ph.D. and Aaron Beck, M.D., I put together my own graphic of what my mother - and these brilliant teachers - taught me. Here's the simple diagram:

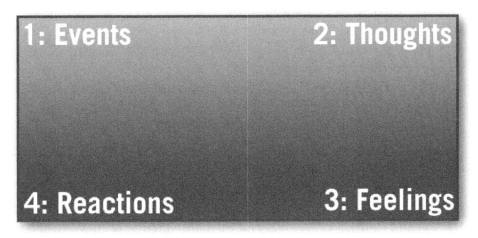

In this box lies the secret sauce to excellence in life whether it is your fitness, your optimal health and wellbeing, relationships, career or wherever you want to sow the seeds of your inborn greatness. I suggest you study it carefully.

See the numbers? They mean something.

1. Position # 1 is filled with all of the situations, conditions, events, people, places, things and events that actually happen in your life.

2. Position # 2 is filled with your *thoughts ABOUT* those events.
3. These thoughts lead directly to, and *fully create*, what's in position # 3, your feelings (some variant of anger, sadness and/or worry on the negative side of the emotional spectrum and love, happiness and tranquility on the positive side).
4. Finally, position # 4 is filled with your reactions/behaviors from the *feelings you created* within yourself resulting from what you *think* in position # 2 about what happens in position # 1.

We never go from an event to an emotion without *thinking* about the event first. It'd be like cutting off your head to think an event *"made you"* or *"got you"* upset. *You never "get" upset by an event*—you create your emotions by what you think about that event. You are not a passive recipient of an emotion—you are an active creator of your emotions. *The link is what you think.*

Here's the important thing: unless and until you *THINK ABOUT* events, you won't have any – *any* – feelings or emotions about events. Do you think if someone shouts, "boo," while you are in a coma, you'd feel fear? No, you wouldn't because you wouldn't be thinking anything about their shouting.

Next time you *"get* scared" (that is, make yourself scared) by a heavy barbell, "feel intimidated" (that is, make yourself intimidated) by a group ex fitness class, "feel overwhelmed" (that is, make yourself feel overwhelmed) by your job responsibilities, or "lose confidence" (that is, make yourself less confident) in your ability to continue on in your studies, ask yourself this:

What am I thinking that's making me feel this way?
Is it **t**rue? Is it **h**elpful? Is it **i**nspirational? Is it **n**ecessary? Is it **k**ind?
See the **THINK** inside those questions?

I suggest you look at this box and examine your thoughts according to my THE LINK IS WHAT YOU THINK model frequently, and see how quickly you learn that you are in total control of your emotions, you are never, ever, "made to" feel something, and you never "get" angry, upset or worried—*you create it all yourself.* That's the all-important step in promoting optimal health and wellbeing and always bringing your best to every situation you face in life.

How? *The link is what you think.* That's how. It's the only way. *The link is what you think.*

Ten Rules to Begin Living Your Best Life

I won't claim these 10 rules are the only rules, the best rules, or the ones that will be best for you to live really well. I've found them to be very helpful. This is an incomplete list, for certain. Give them a chance and see if you derive more pleasure, satisfaction and fulfillment from your life.

1. Why worry? It's the most unproductive thing you can do. It takes as much energy to believe that all will be well as to worry that it won't. Both are predictions, so why live predicting the worst?

2. Why be fearful? Most of the things you fear won't come to pass. Change your perception and you'll stop scaring yourself. The link is always what you think. Apply this favorite saying of mine by Steve Maraboli, "As I look back on my life, I realize that every time I thought I was being rejected from something that I thought was good, I was actually being redirected to something a whole lot better."

3. You can't cross a bridge until you come to it, so don't try. And don't put up your umbrella before it starts raining either. Remember that you often have to go through closed doors to get to an open door.

4. Love, be purposeful, express gratitude, laugh and put family first. Yes, those are more than just one rule. But they are all important.

5. Taking your problems to bed makes for a poor bedfellow. Leave your problems in another room, and you'll sleep better. Turn the page, don't sweat it, don't regret it, move forward and forget it. Create deep, restful sleep for yourself.

6. Other people care for their problems better than you, so don't borrow theirs. And while you're at it, don't let others dictate how you live your life. Delete, unsubscribe and unfriend those who drag you down. You can't live positively with negativity pulling at you.

7. You can't relive yesterday's good or bad, so focus on now. It's best to drive looking through the windshield, not through the rear view mirror. Instead of "I am___" and filling in the blank with negativity, replace those baseless, irrational thoughts with positive ones. Start your day off as positively as you can, ideally with a grateful thought before you get out of bed. Setback? They simply mean you are closer to your dreams being fulfilled.

8. Be as fit and healthy in your mind and body as you can be—proper exercise, wise nutrition and rational thinking all help. So will staying away from anyone who smokes and avoiding any other toxins you can identify. You won't get to 100 if you don't live to 60.

9. Your frustrations and anger are rooted in your insisting that your life _must_, _should_ and _ought_ be different than it is—this is the ultimate obstacle to taking positive steps forward. **_DIE_**... **D**emanding, **I**nsisting and **E**xpecting that life be the way you think it must be is a sure-fire way to, well, **_DIE_**.

10. Develop "regardless thinking," so that no matter what happens in your life—and stuff will--you choose to be happy, nevertheless. That includes problems with money, relationships and jobs. Say "thank you" instead of "but what if..."

Four Essential Links to Bringing Your Best to Your Daily Life

1. *Not everything is possible, but so what?*
   Who says certain outcomes *MUST, OUGHT, HAVE TO,* or *SHOULD* be possible? Give up the demand, insistence or expectation (D.I.E.) that life be a certain way and you've released yourself to enjoy what is, perhaps what was supposed to be, what may have been destined instead, what good may be hiding. Perhaps your belief that something *MUST* be possible is simply erroneous. The JV think to themselves, "Oh, it'll happen if I work harder at it, but maybe not right now." The Varsity say to themselves, "I can be happy and remain positive even if and when things don't work out like I would have wanted or thought they would." The JV are happy only IF things work out the way they want or demand. The Varsity are unconditionally self-accepting and ok regardless of what happens.

2. *Focus on what's going right and be grateful for it*
   I have a belief that is summarized in this acronym, EWOP: Everything works out perfectly! What could be "right" about getting fired from your job? What could be "right" about missing a plane? What could be "right" about a flat tire? What could be "right" about a relationship that went sour?

What could be "right" about a life-threatening diagnosis?
And be GRATEFUL on top of it?

Seriously Michael? Yes, seriously. You know that new job
you have? You know that person you met at the airport on
another flight? You know that traffic jam you avoided? You
know that new guy or gal you've just met? You know how
many friends came out of the woodwork to show their love
and support when they heard about your illness? What do
you want to focus on?

3. *Change is always for the good*
Many people believe, falsely, that change is always for the bad.
When you hear yourself predicting the future based on the
present, especially if that prediction is negative, you are actually "cursing your future." "I'll never pass this course," "I'll
never lose weight," "I'll never meet the right person." You
are filling your mindset with a defeated filter through which
you only see the sour in life, not life's sweetness. We become
comfortable with where we are, with our friends, our job and
sometimes are afraid of change. Remember when Steve Jobs
was fired from Apple, the company he started? He sure could
have thought, " Oh no this is terrible, this change is bad."
He moved forward with the belief that nothing happens TO
you, but rather change happens FOR you. He started another
company, learned new skills, grew the company until it was
so successful that Apple bought it and re-hired Jobs—with a
new set of skills and confidence that led him to create even
greater impact on the world of technology and life. And of
all of the quotes on seeing change as always positive, something better's coming, is this one from Marilyn Monroe, "I
believe that everything happens for a reason. People change
so that you can learn to let go, things go wrong so that you
appreciate them when they're right, you believe in lies so you
eventually learn to trust no one but yourself, and sometimes

good things fall apart so better things can fall together." The point is to accept and grasp change to move forward to your destination.

4. *Leave no room in your mind for anything negative.* Who is living in the vacant spaces of your mind? If you allow negative thoughts in, and don't rid them quickly, you'll find yourself overrun by the kind of voices and weeds that destroy any chance of the good life, happiness or optimism. Do you see yourself defeated, predict loss, see emptiness and sorrow ahead? Or do you visualize and imagine yourself happy, rising, healthy, peaceful, prospering, advancing, being promoted? If you can't even conceive it, you won't believe it. If all you read are lists of sad, depressive, negative stories, use only negative adjectives, science tells us that you'll come to feel that way. What you put in and allow in your life, impacts you, just like the flavor you add to your coffee—chocolate or vanilla. It tastes like what you put into it. Yes, *the link is definitely what you think.*

Yes, the good life can be taught. That means you can learn, which means you are thinking differently. That's where the link is what you think begins...in your thinking. Add these four powerfully positive thoughts to your mindset and watch the good life, happiness and satisfaction emerge. The power is entirely in the words you hear in your self-talk, in your thinking, so begin by changing those words, talking positively to yourself, and unconditionally accepting everything about you.

I'm confident this book can help you sow the seeds of your own inborn greatness, help you find your talents and strengths, and encourage you to appreciate the power of your voice, your thoughts, your self-definition...and your unconditional self-acceptance.

New Year

1. The New Year helps us move to a new address: New Beginnings Blvd.
2. The New Year helps us begin again reaching for anything we want
3. The New Year is the best time for a best new start
4. The New Year helps us become better, not stay bitter
5. The New Year starts a new month, a new year, a new mindset, a new start...will you be open to seeing and savoring it all, or will you go through it all mindlessly?

Action plan

_____

_____

_____

_____

_____

USA (Unconditional Self-Acceptance)

1. When you fully, unconditionally, accept yourself, it doesn't matter to you if the rest of the world does. Sounds pretty healthy to me.
2. Want to feel free, happy, and invincible? Fully, unconditionally, accept yourself.
3. When not achieving your goals affects your unconditional self-acceptance, it's time to rethink the link between the two.
4. When you treat your mind right, you'll feel unconditional self-acceptance. When you don't think well, depression, anger and anxiety may likely result.
5. Instant Band-Aids to build unconditional self-acceptance: "Regardless," "so what?" "Doesn't truly matter," "Who really cares?," "Not going to rate my self."

Action plan

_____
_____
_____
_____
_____

Regardless thinking

1. Since you are in charge of how you feel today, any particular reason you'd make yourself feel less than good?
2. Want to feel good today? Try my frequently applied single word method. It's called "Regardless." Perhaps you prefer my two-word method, "So What?" Apply frequently throughout the day.
3. Get lost in the right direction and see how good that feels.
4. Be aware of what you mean to others, how you've impacted others...wow will you feel good!
5. Feeling good is entirely an inside job—inside your mind and inside your thinking, not inside your wallet.

Action plan

_____
_____
_____
_____
_____

Putting yourself on top

1. Make time to deeply and compassionately value yourself
2. Delete the pills and alcohol to avoid inevitable long-term life-shortening consequences
3. Bring gratitude, positivity and positive people into your life
4. Stop "reducing" and "managing" stress! Instead, learn how to prevent stress in the first place. It's not inevitable. It's in your thinking.
5. Shhh. That means give yourself a chance to hear your deepest thoughts. How? Mindfulness is the best way.

Action plan

_____

_____

_____

_____

_____

Growing

1. Stepping back isn't any more "safe" than stepping forward is "frightening"
   #TheLinkIsWhatYouThink
2. Other people's opinion of your decisions, dreams, even doom have nothing at all to do with you
   #TheLinkIsWhatYouThink
3. Those "reasons" you believe are responsible for you not moving forward are baloney
   #TheLinkIsWhatYouThink
4. The only way you'll grow through what you're going through is...in your mind
   #TheLinkIsWhatYouThink
5. See possibility wherever you are and watch how doors and obstacles vanish
   #TheLinkIsWhatYouThink

Action plan

Your Wellness

1. Not living a healthy lifestyle? How do you talk yourself out of doing so?
2. Your body always tells you what it needs: healthy food, movement, sleep and relationships. Are you listening?
3. Think being fit and well are expensive? Try being ill.
4. Want to lose weight? It's a state of mind. Change your mind change your body
5. When you learn how to not need medicine, you've given yourself the gift of life.

Action plan

_____

_____

_____

_____

_____

Confidence

1. Confidence is quiet. Insecurity is loud.
2. Confidence is comfort being who you want to be, not whom "they" think you "should" be.
3. Confidence is starting later than everyone else, looking different than everyone else, feeling uncertain about you compared to everyone else, and still succeeding.
4. Confidence is running your own race and never comparing yourself to anyone
5. Confidence is talking to you the way you would to someone you love.

Action plan

_____

_____

_____

_____

_____

Generosity

1. Be careful about confusing your generous nature doing for others with other people's unwillingness to do for you. Keep being you, regardless.
2. Takers eventually lose. Givers eternally win.
3. If you believe helping others drives your success you're a giver. If you believe taking from others drives your success you're not a taker, you're a loser.
4. Hi, what can I do for you?
   Hi, what can you do for me?
   You choose.
5. Don't ever be fooled thinking takers, users and brain pickers like you. Watch what happens when they no longer need you. Keep being you, regardless.

Action plan

_____
_____
_____
_____
_____

Talking to yourself?

1. Are you your own worst enemy? If so, check those negative committee meetings in your head and learn how to end those meetings immediately
2. If your mind is negative, your life is too.
3. How do you complete "I am_____."? It'll shape your life, so choose carefully.
4. Imagine if you really stopped yourself from negative self-talk, making excuses and/or giving up. You'd be bringing your best self wherever you go!
5. Catch, challenge and change your negative thoughts to live better. Sure it's easier said than done. You may need another "C" to insure you accomplish this. That "C" is your coach.

Action plan

_____

_____

_____

_____

_____

Mindful?

1. Today, open your hear and your mind. Shhh, hear yourself better now?
2. Your brains won't fall out if you open your mind. You will have greater consciousness, awareness, and attentiveness...ok, and "mindfulness" too
3. Fooled by the "experts" thinking you always need a plan? Nonsense. You need a curious, trusting, open, faith-filled and courageous mind.
4. Today, share what's in your heart more than what is in your mind
5. Happiness lies in your mind fully hearing your heart...not what label you're wearing.

Action plan

_____
_____
_____
_____
_____

Renewal

1. Think differently, feel differently and you've set yourself on the path to renewal.
2. Your real adversity is not the adversity you face, but the adversity you think. It's time for renewed thinking.
3. Think of your renewed mind as a fresh canvas...are you putting more pain or fresh paint on it?
4. See the crispness in the air as a signal to renew your attitude, reset your mindset and rethink your inner critic
5. Renewal often requires failing in a bad place to stand in a better place

Action plan

_____

_____

_____

_____

_____

Improvement

1. You have NOTHING to prove. But like all of us, you have everything to continually improve.
2. One of the really nice things about people, who are on continuous quest for self-improvement, is that they have little or no time to criticize and judge others.
3. When you read books, listen to podcasts, learn a new skill, are always open to change and feedback, spend time helping your community — that's called self-improvement.
4. When you are committed to continuous self-improvement, you reflect an understanding that you aren't a finished product.
5. There is no real success or achievement without a mindset driving actions advancing your continual self-improvement. Otherwise, it's just about beating the other guy.

Action plan

_____
_____
_____
_____
_____

Recovery

1. In order to make room for the things you truly, deeply love, make time for recovery first.
2. Every expenditure of your energy is best met with a recovery period to refuel.
3. Recovery begins with thinking differently about the benefits of genuinely improving and changing...and not.
4. How important is it to you, how confident and ready are you, to change from what you are doing now?
5. The key link between full recovering from anything and staying where you are, is...yep, is what you think.

Action plan

_____
_____
_____
_____
_____

Believe in you

1. When your thoughts are so colored by insecurity, you'll create lies you'll believe to be true
2. See the truth, know the truth and still believe in lies? Stoopid!
3. Want to believe in yourself more than you do? Start by deleting that comparing yourself to others thing you do
4. Believing in others is a remarkable gift that'll bring out the best in them
5. Regardless of who does or doesn't believe in you, you need to believe in your own seeds of greatness. Do you?

Action plan

_____

_____

_____

_____

_____

More regardless thinking

1. Your happiness has nothing to do with anyone or anything else
2. Your happiness is entirely an inside job
3. Looking for someone to "make you happy"? Uhm, look in the mirror. That person is you
4. The assassins of your happiness are comparisons, conditional thinking, seeking perfection and demanding change
5. You can live happily by choosing to house happy thoughts. After all, yep, "The link is what you think."

Action plan

_____
_____
_____
_____
_____

Living Well

1. Live simply — materialism really doesn't matter and like fame and hedonism, doesn't lead to happiness
2. Accept yourself unconditionally, and you'll be better able to accept others and life, especially those things you cannot control and those people who won't change
3. It's all temporary so what are you fretting about?
4. You are never, ever, a victim of others. Learn to recognize that being so, is only in your thoughts. You are always the victor when seen through the lens of growing and learning from every situation.
5. You can always optimize and maximize positive feelings. Practice "Regardless" "So what?" "Who cares?" thinking.

Action plan

_____
_____
_____
_____
_____

Be you

1. Are you the same person personally and publicly?
2. Doesn't it take more energy to be phony than to be genuine?
3. To be authentic, genuine, means ripping up fear of what others may think.
4. Eliminate competition from your life by running your own race, eliminate all comparison and simply be your authentic, genuine self.
5. Want to avoid failure? Just be you. You can't fail if you're simply genuine.

Action plan

_____

_____

_____

_____

_____

Healthy?

1. When you fully, unconditionally, accept yourself, it doesn't matter to you if the rest of the world does. Sounds pretty healthy to me.
2. Want to feel free, happy and invincible? Fully, unconditionally, accept yourself.
3. When not achieving your goals affects your unconditional self-acceptance, it's time to rethink the link between the two.
4. When you treat your mind right, you'll feel unconditional self-acceptance. When you don't think well, depression, anger and anxiety may likely result.
5. Instant Band-Aids to build unconditional self-acceptance: "regardless," "so what?" "It doesn't truly matter," "who really cares?," "not going to rate my self."

Action plan

_____
_____
_____
_____
_____

What Matters

1. A key to happiness is to no longer confuse what & who doesn't matter with what & who does
2. Want to reduce stress? Give less attention to thinking it's important when it really isn't
3. If you believe they "must" like you, you've made yourself their victim. You, not them, did that to you.
4. Looking for a sign of maturity? If you find drama, you haven't found that sign yet
5. If you've searched the Internet for those who give a sh#$ and your name isn't there, congratulations

Action plan

_____
_____
_____
_____
_____

Angry?

1. So you are angry. What the heck does that have to do with you being cruel to anyone else?
2. Grow up. Nobody, "makes you angry" and nobody "pisses you off." Only you make you angry because you continue to Demand, Insist and Expect (D.I.E.) that others act the way you think they must.
3. The angriest people I've ever known are the ones who've been hurt early in life and have never successfully dealt with it.
4. Want to be an enemy of yourself, of your own happiness and your wellbeing? React with anger at others whenever possible.
5. When you feel pain, choose another reaction or response besides anger. How about admitting your pain and dealing with that instead?

Action plan

_____

_____

_____

_____

_____

Seriously, so what?

1. So they're judging you unfairly. So what? Seriously, so what?
2. So they're gossiping about you. So what? Seriously, so what?
3. So it's really hard. So what? Seriously, so what?
4. So it didn't work out like you had hoped. So what? Seriously, so what?
5. So you made a mistake. So what? Seriously, so what?

Action plan

_____
_____
_____
_____
_____

Ready to advance?

1. Don't ever let perfection impede your advancement and joy
2. Embrace every change that comes your way, with curiosity and gratitude for what it'll bring for you
3. Recognize that all motivation is self-motivation. Nobody ever really motivates you. Only you do
4. Live now, not through the rear view mirror.
5. Never ever take offense. Why bother? Give another that power over you? Not ever

Action plan

_____

_____

_____

_____

_____

Clear thinking

1. Are your grateful for your stumbling blocks? You would be if your vision were set right.
2. Obstacles may not be the path, but they sure can show you better paths
3. See obstacles like barbells. The heavier you lift, the stronger you become.
4. Obstacles don't define or destroy you. Only you do.
5. Unless you have a mind cramp, a bump in the road no matter how harsh, won't derail you.

Action plan

_____

_____

_____

_____

_____

Controlling your mind

1. Can you view the insulting words of another as "just words"? Use their shoddy behavior to learn...to speak with others in kind and respectful ways.
2. Remember that no matter where you mind is, you are always in the present. That's where your power to self-correct lies, in the now.
3. Sages ask, "Who is an honorable person?" They answer, "The one who shows honor and respect to others." Do you?
4. Your facial expression gives it all away. The only way for your expression to fully change is for you to change your inner thoughts about another. Don't, and see how your conscious mind won't control all of your facial muscles.
5. Inner calm will help you speak with others in a calm way, promoting harmony between you and others.

Action plan

_____

_____

_____

_____

_____

Judgments

1. It's always easier to judge the mistakes of others than our own.
2. They don't define you by their judgments. You define you by your thoughts.
3. They're entitled to their opinion of you. You're entitled to completely ignore them.
4. Ever realize that people who truly understand you don't judge you and people who judge you have no understanding of you?
5. What's their opinion and judgment of you actually have to do with you? Nothing. The link is what you think.

Action plan

_____

_____

_____

_____

_____

True Beauty

1. Do you always find beauty in others? That's a sign that you are a beautiful person.
2. Are you able to appreciate character flaws? That's a sign that you are a beautiful person.
3. Who really cares about how attractive someone is on the outside? Isn't it what's in one's heart that really counts?
4. Do you really buy those so obviously photo shopped cosmetic before and after sales pitches? Look beyond the outside to that which lies within. That's where beauty lies.
5. Calling someone else "ugly" doesn't make you attractive. Far, far, from it.

Action plan

_____

_____

_____

_____

_____

Goal digger?

1. Do you have a goal that'll spark you to jump out of bed?
2. What's it going to take to turn yourself into a goal digger?
3. Want to stretch? Keep your goals out of reach, but not out of sight.
4. When you feel uncomfortable telling small-minded people about your goals, you know you've set them large enough
5. Set HARD goals, not SMART goals...heartfelt, animated, required and difficult

Action plan

_____

_____

_____

_____

_____

Acceptance 101

1. How's all that "shoulding" doing for your mood?
2. Want to improve your mood? Let each situation be what it is instead of what you fervently believe it "should" be.
3. Dealing with someone you think is a fool? The best response is silence. Yours. Not theirs.
4. Instead of tripping over the shit in your life, why not simply walk over it?
5. Do everything with kindness and see how it improves your life.

Action plan

_____

_____

_____

_____

_____

Shhh...

1. Talk too much and they'll think you're a fool. Be silent and they'll be curious.
2. Another's silence has nothing to do with your worth.
3. Isn't it terrific when you remain silent when others expect you to be enraged?
4. I find that the most confident talk the least while the most insecure talk the most.
5. The more you listen to yourself, the more wisdom and inspiration you'll find.

Action plan

_____

_____

_____

_____

_____

Try honesty

1. Wouldn't you prefer honesty to sugar-coated bullsh#$?
2. You may not get a whole lot of friends being honest, but you'll sure get the right ones
3. Rather be impressive than honest? Pffff, just keep walking.
4. Proverbs teaches, "The first step towards greatness is to be honest"
5. Want to be trusted? Tell, speak, live and love honesty.

Action plan

_____
_____
_____
_____
_____

Drop these

1. Will you neglect any opportunities for self-improvement today? What'd be your excuse if you do?
2. What are you creating for yourself today?
3. That mistake you will make today, it's meant for learning, not repeating.
4. I've just revoked your permission to live with fear today—it's holding you back from reaching your dreams.
5. Forget about being superior to others—just focus on being superior to how you were yesterday.

Action plan

_____
_____
_____
_____
_____

Getting along?

1. Yesterday leadership meant muscle. Today it means getting along with people.
2. Want to get along with people? Don't demand, insist or expect them to be like you (D.I.E.).
3. Trying to get along with others? Be sure you get along with yourself first.
4. Want to get along with yourself? Don't let others who do little or nothing for you, control your mind and feelings.
5. The formula of success, the not so secret ingredient, depends first on getting along with others.

Action plan

_____
_____
_____
_____
_____

Stuck in a rut?

1. Stuck in a rut? Question everything but your ability to get unstuck.
2. Stuck in a rut? You aren't. You only THINK you are. Change your thoughts and you're rut will change.
3. Stuck in a rut? Wish you weren't? Stop wishing. Start moving.
4. Stuck in a rut? This is not where your story must end—you can bust through.
5. Stuck in a rut? Stop believing it and thus keeping it an obstacle.

Action plan

_____
_____
_____
_____
_____

You won't get it done by...

1. You won't get it done just by talking.
2. You won't get it done by waiting for the right moment, condition or for assistance.
3. You won't get it done continuously playing someone else's games.
4. You won't get it done refusing to do something you've never done before.
5. You won't get it done by accepting "almost done."

Action plan

_____

_____

_____

_____

_____

Want to transform yourself?

1. Want to transform yourself? What small choices and successes are you building over time?
2. Want to transform yourself? Get your inside game right before you focus on your score.
3. Want to transform yourself? Be truthfully and fully ready to reassess, redefine and then remold yourself.
4. Want to transform yourself? Stay in the present. That's where transformative activity occurs.
5. Want to transform yourself? The obstacle, challenge and/ or frustration you are facing are golden opportunities for self-transformation.

Action plan

_____
_____
_____
_____
_____

Judging others is a waste of your time

1. Look in the mirror. That's your competition.
2. Judging others? You aren't defining them. You are defining you.
3. Success. It's always the best revenge. That and of course, moving forward.
4. Let karma do its job. Unless someone bothers your family. Then you become karma.
5. Sorry to let you know, but when you were busy judging others, your skeletons fell out of your closet.

Action plan

_____
_____
_____
_____
_____

Wasting your time?

1. Want to insure you aren't ever happy? Constantly worry about what others think about you.
2. Want to insure you are always someone's prisoner? Care a lot about what he/she thinks about you.
3. What others think about you is really none of your business.
4. You might worry less about what others think about you if you realized how seldom they do—and how it makes absolutely no difference.
5. Maybe all that worry about what others think of you is really just worrying about what you think of you.

Action plan

_____

_____

_____

_____

_____

Lack of confidence

1. No confidence? No worries. You'll find a way not to win.
2. Know the difference between winning and losing? Not quitting.
3. Don't see yourself as a winner? You won't perform as one either.
4. The science of winning is simple. Be thoroughly prepared.
5. Winners are wise when they lose and happy when they win.

Action plan

_____

_____

_____

_____

_____

Gossiping?

1. Ever notice how people are ready to believe the bad about others?
2. People who gossip are trying to avoid their own pain.
3. Your tongue weighs practically nothing. So why can't you hold it?
4. Imagine thanking people who gossip about you. For what? For making you the center of their world.
5. Can you give your pet parrot to a gossiper?

Action plan

_____

_____

_____

_____

_____

Friendship

1. Making hundreds of friends is not a miracle. The miracle is to make a friend who stands by you when hundreds are against you.
2. Misfortune helps...in identifying who your real friends are.
3. You never lose a real friend. Think about that.
4. Need defines friendship. Real friends are always there when you need them. Fake friends are there only when they need you.
5. Beliefs define friendship. Genuine friends believe in you. Phony friends believe rumors.

Action plan

_____

_____

_____

_____

_____

Want to be happy?

1. Want to be happy? Free your heart from demands and expectations.
2. Want to be happy? Free your thoughts from the future, and savor this moment.
3. Want to be happy? Free your space from excess, and simplify.
4. Want to be happy? Free yourself from your need to be seen by others in a certain way.
5. Want to be happy? Free your life from people who try to drag you down.

Action plan

_____
_____
_____
_____
_____

Kindness

1. Want to connect with the deaf and blind? Mark Twain suggested that we try kindness.
2. Not sure if a situation calls for you to be right or to be kind? Don't be silly. Choose kindness.
3. You don't really think you need a reason to help someone do you?
4. Kindness does have side effects: a healthy heart, better relationships, increased joy, it's anti-aging and it's contagious.
5. Kindness — it'll bless the giver and the receiver.

Action plan

_____

_____

_____

_____

_____

Do you...?

1. Do you collect things or experiences?
2. Do you know the price of everything and the value of nothing?
3. Do you know how much you'd be worth if you lost all of your money?
4. Do you raise your kids to "have more" than you or to "be more" than you?
5. Do you know that having everything you desire is not normal?

Action plan

_____
_____
_____
_____
_____

Going forward?

1. When people walk away from you, don't stop them. Their part in your story is over.
2. You'll arrive when, and with whom, you are supposed to. Not one minute sooner or later. And not with anyone else.
3. Sometimes you'll need a door to close to propel you forward. Trust your time to move ahead.
4. If Cinderella went back to pick up her shoe, she wouldn't have become a princess. Keep looking forward.
5. Want to amaze yourself? Just keep moving forward.

Action plan

_____

_____

_____

_____

_____

Going in the right direction

1. Turn your problems into guidelines, not stop signs
2. Keep making mistakes and stop faking perfection.
3. Regrets? No. You either win or you learn.
4. The best steering wheels in life are your thoughts—they'll move you in the direction you choose.
5. Forget those that derail you and focus on those that regale you.

Action plan

_____

_____

_____

_____

_____

Respect

1. I respect those who've earned it and who deserve it, never those who demand it. Never. Ever.
2. Don't give away your self-respect, dignity and self-regard trying to make others respect and appreciate you—especially when they are put together in a way that leaves them unable to do so.
3. There's a difference between cutting people out of your life and hating them. It's all about respecting you first.
4. Insult someone and watch what happens. The only thing that changes is the respect they have for you.
5. When respect is anchored in fear, it's not respect. It's despicable.

Action plan

_____

_____

_____

_____

_____

What matters now?

1. You know what really matters? Think about time—it'll show you what really matters
2. When you look back at it now, you probably wonder why you made such a big deal about it, right?
3. Isn't it interesting that as you've gotten older, what others think or say about you matters so little?
4. Who you used to be, truly, doesn't matter at all. What matters is who you are becoming.
5. So, at this point in your life, have your figured out who really matters, who never did and always will?

Action plan

_____
_____
_____
_____
_____

Making a difference

1. Want to make a difference? Care - really care - for another.
2. But what if the other person doesn't care back? Who cares?
3. I like what Margaret Mead said about caring, "Never believe that a few caring people can't change the world. For, indeed, all who ever have."
4. Try this today: do one act of caring that will likely have no reciprocation...amazing, right?
5. Care about the happiness of others, within reason, and you'll realize your own.

Action plan

_____

_____

_____

_____

_____

Who are you?

1. What you think you are NOT is what's keeping you from advancing.
2. What are you getting out of spending your time worrying about what others think of you?
3. Stop wanting to be someone else. It's impossible and thus ridiculous.
4. What good comes to you from judging yourself through the eyes of others?
5. Don't waste a moment of your day being against yourself.

Action plan

_____

_____

_____

_____

_____

What's more important?

1. People before things.
2. Your insides and other people's outsides - never, ever, compare these.
3. Create challenging and achievable goals daily.
4. Don't look at your bank account or possessions to define your success.
5. Made a mistake? Screw up? I know someone who was fired from a newspaper because he had no imagination or original ideas. Didn't stop Walt Disney. Don't let your setbacks be anything but set ups to comeback. Always.

Action plan

_____

_____

_____

_____

_____

Promoting you

1. Don't believe your imagined fears are real.
2. Compare & despair. Comparing yourself to others or to other times in your life will prevent you from moving forward.
3. Start your day with a direction, a plan and a goal.
4. Replace "what if" with "so what?"
5. Forget achieving perfection and instead strive to be resilient.

Action plan

_____
_____
_____
_____
_____

Fear...yuchhh

1. Want to overcome fear? It'll take action more than thought.
2. Fearful? What's the story you are telling yourself? That's where your fear is born.
3. Try replacing fear with genuine curiosity. It changes the whole experience.
4. Faith trumps fear.
5. Instead of living your fear, live your hopes and dreams.

Action plan

_____

_____

_____

_____

_____

Do you believe?

1. Do you believe in the magic of kindness?
2. Do you believe that kindness can ever be wasted?
3. Do you believe that kindness is the most valuable gift you can ever give to another?
4. Do you believe that one act of kindness can change an entire day for another?
5. Do you believe that it is always possible to be kind?

Action plan

_____
_____
_____
_____
_____

Motivating questions

1. Do you spend more time lifting yourself up or putting others down?
2. Who did you last gossip about, how do you feel about it now?
3. When did you last say "thank you" and sincerely mean it?
4. Do you practice 'self love' or 'self loathing'?
5. What answers are you seeking about your life?

Action plan

_____
_____
_____
_____
_____

Laughing yet?

1. If laughter is the best medicine, and exercise is medicine too, why not laugh while exercising?
2. Need a quick vacation right where you are? Try laughter. See????
3. Your sense of humor is you—don't apologize for it.
4. Laugh at what you stress about and you'll be amazed how that stress will fade.
5. Want to waste a day of your life? Don't laugh for the next 24 hours.

Action plan

_____
_____
_____
_____
_____

Faith

1. Is your faith bigger than your fear?
2. Faith in yourself means worrying little about whom else has faith in you.
3. Starve your fear...feed your faith.
4. Let your faith brighten your future.
5. Faith, trust with no reservation, is the only fuel that ultimately moves you forward.

Action plan

_____

_____

_____

_____

_____

Sensitivity

1. Don't confuse being sensitive to others with weakness. It's actually compassion.
2. Sensitive? It only means you have the ability to mean what you say when you say, "I understand how you feel."
3. Think you are "too sensitive"? No, it's just that every word and action goes to your heart.
4. When your feelings are hurt it's not necessarily that you are being too sensitive, it may mean the other person is not at all sensitive.
5. Other people's feelings mean nothing to you? Be careful, it could mean a whole lot to them.

Action plan

_____

_____

_____

_____

_____

What's fair?

1. Spread your "rain" on others to help them grow. "Rain" = Acting with fairness.
2. Everyone wants to lose weight. Don't forget about the benefits of losing fair-weather friends.
3. Nope, life is not fair. Never was supposed to be and never will be. Deal with it.
4. Life "unfair" to you? Nothing will drive others crazier than seeing you living a good life regardless.
5. The only place fairness resides for certain is within you. Give it away with no fairy tale expectation that you'll get it back.

Action plan

_____

_____

_____

_____

_____

Do you?

1. Do you have confidence in what your children can accomplish? The right answer is "Of course I do, Yes."
2. Do you feel "entitled" to things you struggled and sweated for? The right answer is No, of course not.
3. Do you focus on milestones or magical moments? The right answer is the Magical Moments—that's all that life is. What's entitled?
4. Do you really believe that "good luck" comes from hard work? The right answer is Duh, of course not. What's good luck?
5. Do you really enjoy the good fortune of others? The right answer is Absolutely, Yes

Action plan

_____

_____

_____

_____

_____

Life worth living

1. Want a life worth living? Start by believing it is.
2. Want something you don't yet have? Stop believing you can't have it.
3. Don't believe in make believe. Believe you can and will make it happen.
4. Believe there's always hope. The alternative path is dismal.
5. Finish this, "I believe with complete faith that_____."

Action plan

_____

_____

_____

_____

_____

Meditate

1. Want to be more you? Meditate.
2. Want to hear more? Quiet your mind and meditate.
3. Bored sitting around doing nothing? Meditate.
4. Want to react to life's difficulties better than you have? Don't simply relax. Meditate.
5. Google not able to answer your questions? Meditate. The answers will appear.

Action plan

_____
_____
_____
_____
_____

Looking for...?

1. Looking for glory? Take the risk and begin moving.
2. Looking for the success formula? It's simple: consistent, relentless, small daily efforts
3. Looking for a guarantee that success will remain? Faggedabowdit.
4. Looking for the key to happiness and think it'll be success? Nope. It's the other way around.
5. Looking for the elevator to success? Stop looking. Take the stairs.

Action plan

_____

_____

_____

_____

_____

Transforming?

1. Want to transform? Start with a daily purposeful change. What's it going to be today?
2. Want to transform? It's not in your future. It's in your immediate now. Go!
3. Are you confusing information with transformation? Stop gathering and act.
4. Transformation is an inside job. Don't look beyond your thoughts.
5. If you enjoy a good mystery, you'll savor the never ending, always evolving twists and turns of life's transformation.

Action plan

_____

_____

_____

_____

_____

Fear and courage

1. Forget hiding from danger. Be fearless.
2. Master your fears and you'll be a role model of courage.
3. Nobody has the promise of succeeding. Only the courageous try anyway.
4. The more at peace and accepting of yourself on the inside, the more you'll display courage on the outside.
5. Have the courage to do what others say you can't.

Action plan

_____

_____

_____

_____

_____

Want to be happy?

1. Want to be happy? Eagerly enjoy trying something new.
2. Want to be happy?
   Run your own race and never, ever, look for validation outside of yourself.
3. Want to be happy?
   Focus on what's going right every moment, every day.
4. Want to be happy?
   Celebrate the success and happiness of others.
5. Want to be happy?
   See rejection as true redirection, setbacks as simply set ups for comebacks, and thrive on challenges.

Action plan

_____

_____

_____

_____

_____

Now

1. Now. That's really all we have. Now. Not then. Now.
2. See the joy and satisfaction in this moment? No? Look wiser. It's there. It'd be a shame to blame not seeing it in someone else.
3. Uh oh. Guess who's listening when you speak? You are! Speak victory, not defeat. No matter what.
4. Those limiting thoughts that are sabotaging you? Detach from them completely, accept what is in front of you with complete unconditional regard and be completely non-judgmental.
5. Now sigh. This is mindful peace.

Action plan

_____
_____
_____
_____
_____

Leadership

1. Think being a leader comes from a title or position? Nope. It comes from being an example.
2. Leadership test: do you inspire or dominate?
3. The deeper ingredients of a leader: happiness, positivity, authenticity and peacefulness.
4. A true leader finds a way to create cooperation, doesn't thrive on divisiveness.
5. Blame something external for stumbling or not advancing? A real leader never stoops that low.

Action plan

_____

_____

_____

_____

_____

Hearing voices?

1. The absence of illness isn't the goal. Complete physical, mental and social wellbeing is.
2. Are you going to be the reason others smile today?
3. Watch what your mind says. Your body is listening.
4. Be careful with your negative voice. It'll talk you right out of your dreams.
5. When your mouth is poor, you're life will be as well.

Action plan

_____
_____
_____
_____
_____

Humor

1. Have you realized yet that a sense of humor makes you more attractive than even plastic surgery?
2. Exercise isn't the only medicine. A good sense of humor is wonderful preventative and curative medicine.
3. Want to speak a truly universal language? Try humor. It'll work every time.
4. Facing some problems? A good sense of humor is a wonderful defense and will get you through it.
5. Lose your sense of humor and you've lost everything.

Action plan

_____
_____
_____
_____
_____

Friendship

1. You know what's good about difficult times? They uncover your real friends.
2. Have someone who knows how crazy you really are and still hangs with you? That'd be a best friend.
3. Those people who talk nicely behind your back...yep, those are your friends.
4. Ever hear of "fake shadow friends"? They follow you in the sun and disappear in the dark.
5. Whether they come for a reason or stay a season, they are your friends. Treat them well.

Action plan

_____

_____

_____

_____

_____

Too busy?

1. "Too busy" is a total myth...if you want to do something you do.
2. Isn't it time to stop glorifying "too busy"?
3. Are you busy with what you "get to do" or with what you "have to do"? Surprise: It's all the way you think about it.
4. When you stay in your quiet place long enough, have you ever thought that your life has been a jumble of busy nothings?
5. If you are a busybody, your work will never be done. Now, that's unfortunate.

Action plan

_____

_____

_____

_____

_____

What's holding you back?

1. The only thing holding you back is your own story of insecurity.
2. Ever find yourself jealous of others? Time to boost your self-confidence story. At those times, it's lacking.
3. Self-confidence is a story you tell yourself about yourself. Ready to begin telling yourself that story right now?
4. "They" telling you a story about you that's designed to pull you down? Tell yourself a different, self-confident, story about yourself that's designed to pull you up.
5. You are a work in progress, not a finished product. Begin speaking a victory story about yourself, stop talking defeat, and soon you'll be wearing the invisible smile of self-confidence.

Action plan

_____

_____

_____

_____

_____

Mindset

1. Do you have the mindset, the mental strength, of a champion? Why not, aren't you a champion?
2. Do you believe your mind is your greatest strength and you are invincible? How do you stop yourself from believing that?
3. Are you holding on to what others think about you while trying to succeed? Uhm, better rethink that.
4. Try this: reveal your sabotaging paradigms; rewrite them to enable you to renew your self-compassion and inner esteem.
5. Are you focusing only on what you can control? You will if you want to transform the way you handle pressure and adversity and successfully rebound from failure.

Action plan

_____

_____

_____

_____

_____

What kind of person are you?

1. Are you a "hope and expectancy" or a "defeat and it'll never happen" person?
2. Are you a "nevertheless and regardless" or a "stop and stuck here" person?
3. Are you an "I get to" or an "I have to" person?
4. Are you a "this is a set up" or a "this is a setback" person?
5. Are you a "happens to me" or a "happens for me" person?

Action plan

_____

_____

_____

_____

_____

Are you...?

1. Are you often looking for someone to tell you that you aren't wrong?
2. Are you often looking for someone to tell you that you are the victim?
3. Are you often looking for someone to help you grow by driving forward clearly?
4. Are you often looking for someone to help you get back on track to continue your upward growth?
5. If you answered "yes" to #s 1 and 2, be smart. Don't waste your time and money on coaching. You aren't ready for it :-)

Action plan

_____

_____

_____

_____

_____

Never give up

1. Ever go against someone who never gives up? Why isn't that YOU?
2. What do circumstances have to do with you achieving your peak performance? Nothing.
3. "FAIL" to someone who is a peak performer means "first attempt in learning."
4. To perform at your peak requires passion, principles and purpose...lock in on yours.
5. Trying to perform at your peak without "imagineering" it first too often leads to failure.

Action plan

_____
_____
_____
_____
_____

Faggedabowdem

1. Your light too bright for someone who's busy trying to dim it? Faggedabowdem
2. People who are intimidated by your present keep bringing up your past? Faggedabowdem
3. Invite people into your home and find that stuff is missing...like hope, peace, happiness and joy? Faggedabowdem
4. You know those people who keep hurting you and still keep expecting you to love them? Faggedabowdem
5. You know those "askholes" who constantly ask for your advice but always does the opposite of what you suggest? Faggedabowdem

Action plan

_____

_____

_____

_____

_____

Success

1. First rule of being successful is to believe you <u>can</u> be & <u>will</u> be.
2. Waiting for conditions to be just right for your success? Don't wait. Create them instead.
3. Failing inspires or defeats - all depends on your mindset program.
4. You breathe without thinking about being successful in breathing. You just do it. Could it be the same in other areas of life?
5. Just do what you love. It'll be successful. Like breathing.

Action plan

_____
_____
_____
_____
_____

Unplug

1. Unplugged for two days. Ahhhh...all working better than before.
2. Unplugging leads to quiet time restoring focus and composure.
3. Unplugging recharges batteries than anything else invented.
4. Unplugging improves hearing...quieter you become, the better you hear.
5. Your turn..."I unplug to_____."

Action plan

_____

_____

_____

_____

_____

What's in your heart?

1. J oy in your heart? That means you've got gratitude inside of you crating your joy.
2. Fill your heart with melody wherever you go, no matter what's going on in the natural.
3. Don't become used to being without joy...you'll only cause yourself needless misery, and imprison yourself with your mind full of resentment, hatred and envy.
4. Move toward a meaningful destination, along a correct path, against resistance and you are on your way to joy.
5. Your external actions can have an effect on your inner feelings, so act "as if" you already have joy and you'll help create it.

Action plan

_____

_____

_____

_____

_____

Simple Wisdom

1. Are you wise enough to walk away from nonsense around you?
2. Nature and wisdom are always aligned. Open your eyes to see that and learn.
3. Want to gain wisdom? Know what you know and don't know.
4. What to say is one thing. When to say it is another. One is knowledge. The other is wisdom. Wise enough to figure out which is which?
5. Be wise enough to not allow someone to waste your time twice.

Action plan

_____

_____

_____

_____

_____

Decisions

1. Trying to make a decision without knowing your values? Forget it.
2. So, you really believe it's your circumstances that have made you? Forget it. It's your decisions.
3. Making a decision you think will make you happy? Forget it. You make yourself happy about your decisions. Uhm, you do, don't you?
4. When you make a decision, there'll be plenty of folks who will guide you who don't have to deal with the results. Forget them... and their advice.
5. Made a difficult decision but can comfortably say, "To me this was the right decision"? Forget it. Your heart's at peace-it was the right decision.

Action plan

_____

_____

_____

_____

_____

The royal "we"

1. Isn't the centerpiece of all wellbeing, the best medicine, really authentic togetherness?
2. Replace "I" in illness with "We" and you've discovered wellness.
3. Do it together, with genuine hope, love and joy...and see how much more you accomplish.
4. Want to say nothing together? Try holding hands...
5. Want to build togetherness? Only see each other's souls...not their bodies, their shape, their size or their words.

Action plan

_____

_____

_____

_____

_____

Togetherness

1. Looking for victory?
   Try creating unity first. It'll lead you to your goal.
2. You are only as strong as you are united with others. Lifting weights won't do it.
3. Turn "me" upside down and you have "we"
4. Looking for happiness? Unity is the key ingredient. Divisiveness will destroy your happiness.
5. Unity isn't the same as uniformity. Don't worry...be yourself with others.

Action plan

_____

_____

_____

_____

_____

Game playing

1. Believe in something but don't live it? Check your authenticity.
2. Honest leaders will create companies that are trustworthy. Manipulative leaders will create companies that are unreliable and irresponsible.
3. Have a phone with no service? You just play games with it. Sort of like what happens with immature leaders who have no trust.
4. Isn't it strange that fake leaders don't surprise people anymore, while it's the loyal ones that do?
5. Immature leaders wish you the best, as long as that best benefits them.

Action plan

_____

_____

_____

_____

_____

Insecure?

1. Insecure in yourself? That'll explain why you talk down so many others.
2. Try to hide your flaws, scarcity mindset, know it all, always seeking validation? It is just insecurity. Sad thing is...everyone sees it.
3. Crumbling position, trying to appear confident but your lifelong insecurity just overwhelms you? Hmm, maybe that's why you insult so many.
4. The six "C's" of insecurity: comparison, compensation, competition, compulsion, condemnation & control.
5. Backstabbers aren't strong, clever, savvy or successful. They are simply insecure.

Action plan

_____

_____

_____

_____

_____

Motivation

1. Here's a good motivation. Your limitations.
2. Oh, you didn't win today? Well if you learned, you won.
3. Want something you've never had? Try doing something you've never done.
4. Some people have never dreamed of success. They've just worked for it.
5. When talent doesn't work hard, hard work beat's talent.

Action plan

_____

_____

_____

_____

_____

Inspiring others

1. Want to inspire others? No need to be perfect. They can be inspired by how you deal with your imperfections.
2. Inspiring others is success. Not what you have or what you accomplish yourself.
3. Live your best version of you and you'll be an inspiration for others to live their best version of themselves.
4. Want to feel inspired? Inspire others.
5. "Because of you I didn't give up..." Great words one can hear.

Action plan

_____
_____
_____
_____
_____

Ahh, harmony

1. Create harmony and be at peace with yourself—your inner light will shine through.
2. With harmony, insignificant things increase and without it significant things melt away.
3. Move in harmony with- not against - yourself, flow, and see how much more magical life will be.
4. Whatever you are thinking affects the world. Please think harmony—it affects us all around you.
5. Want to avoid being distracted by doubts, destructive thoughts, and worry? Move into the still, quiet eye of the hurricane, where you can more easily focus on harmony.

Action plan

_____
_____
_____
_____
_____

Sagacity

1. Want your team to succeed while others around fail? Build a transformative team where everyone's voice is equally meritorious, everyone's input equally valued and heard, and everyone's empowered to achieve.
2. Do you listen more or talk more? It'll determine the success of your team and if members follow you. Combined effort of every member makes the difference.
3. Is your team winning or just listening? Trust, respect, understand and enjoy…that's T.E.A.M.
4. Are your team meetings just opportunities for you to blab on and on without listening to anyone? Inspire or expire.
5. Every individual member of a team can make a pivotal difference, but a single member of a team can't make a team.

Action plan

_____
_____
_____
_____
_____

Who's against you?

1. Never, ever give up. That's what they're hoping you'll do. Succeed for the people who want you to fail.
2. Make your goals so resolute that hindrances, stumbles, setbacks and failures are nothing but pure motivation.
3. What's following your "I am..." today? Chose wisely, since that's what'll be staring you in the face tomorrow. Try this "I am..." "I am ready for whatever comes my way."
4. Those who are acting like it's them against you, and maybe even the world, are really only acting against themselves. They just keep comparing and despairing, trying to appear confident in their crumbling position.
5. Ever notice that an insecure narrow mind and a big mouth frequently go together? They have to have the last word. So what? Let them, smile to yourself and keep succeeding.

Action plan

_____

_____

_____

_____

_____

What are you focusing on?

1. Treat life like a camera. Focus on who and what's important. Delete the rest.
2. Give time the opportunity to show you who and what's important.
3. Want to know what's important? Be a voice, not an echo.
4. You define important, not them.
5. What you focus on is far more important than how intelligent you may be.

Action plan

_____

_____

_____

_____

_____

You or them?

1. You can either be happy or care about what others think about you, but not both.
2. The less you care what others think about you, the happier you'll be.
3. Caring about what others think, say, or gossip about you is detrimental to your health.
4. Spend today, and tomorrow, being yourself in a world that persists in trying to make you into something else...your confidence will soar.
5. Who are you living for? Them, or you?

Action plan

_____

_____

_____

_____

_____

Your inner strengths

1. Looking for strength? You'll find it primarily inside of you, more than inside of a gym.
2. Those difficulties you are facing aren't destructive. They come to show you your inner strength, your potential, your power.
3. No struggle? Then there'll be no strength. Overcoming what you think you thought you couldn't builds your inner strength.
4. There's turbocharged fuel inside of your tank that you think is empty. You're filled with inner strength!
5. It's time to liberate your inner strength...what are you waiting for?

Action plan

_____

_____

_____

_____

_____

Success begins with...

1. Success and action are linked. Not likely to have one without the other. Are you still moving or giving up?
2. When you want to succeed as much as you want to put out the fire in your hair, you'll be successful.
3. Success begins with a mindset of succeeding. Repeat: "I am successful." Now repeat: "I am a failure." Which one echoes most between your ears and behind your eyes?
4. Success won't bring authentic happiness. But happiness may just be the fuel to lead you to success.
5. Don't love what you do? Hmm, and you still think you'll be successful in it? Er, uhm, better rethink that one.

Action plan

_____
_____
_____
_____
_____

So they do...

1. People will talk about you, of course. They can't stand your success. Smile and succeed over their whispers.
2. People try to rain on your parade only because they desire the sun shining on you and dislike the shade they're standing in. Put on sunglasses and keep succeeding.
3. Someone rude to you? Fageddabowdit—it's only their poor imitation of strength. Don't interrupt your success by even noticing how pathetic they are.
4. Being belittled by someone? That means they're feeling threatened by your success and skills. Yep, keep succeeding—their feeling threatened is their misery, not yours.
5. They ignore you because they see your potential as a threat to their success. Good they are ignoring you so you're not distracted from succeeding.

Action plan

_____

_____

_____

_____

_____

You, yourself and your life

1. Listen to others and then trust yourself
2. Be a good boss to yourself
3. Make your own rules - be the flipper, not the pinball
4. It takes longer than you think, so have patience
5. Say "no" without guilt

Action plan

_____

_____

_____

_____

_____

Smile

1. Ever notices how one smile starts because of another?
2. Use your smile to help change the world, just don't let the world change your smile.
3. S.M.I.L.E. = See miracles in life everywhere
4. The best way to live? Smile and forgive.
5. When you smile it'll either warm them up or piss them off. Who cares? You win :-) either way.

Action plan

_____

_____

_____

_____

_____

Your thoughts

1. Your life is what your thoughts make it
2. Your body hears your thoughts. Be careful to stay positive
3. Never, ever, let what's going on outside affect what's going on inside
4. Your mindset is everything
5. Because the other person is miserable is no reason for you to be

Action plan

_____
_____
_____
_____
_____

Silence...shhhh

1. The day you are silent about what really matters, your life will begin to fade.
2. What's continuing in your life is what you are allowing in your life.
3. Standing alone when you're standing for what's right? So what? Stand there.
4. Ohhh, so some people don't like you? Just means you've stood for something in life.
5. Stand up for yourself even if nobody else is on your side.

Action plan

_____

_____

_____

_____

_____

Don't fear being creative

1. Fear you'll be wrong? Stop trying to be creative. Can't have both.
2. Think of a problem as the alarm going off to awaken your creativity.
3. Want to think more efficiently? Try thinking creatively. Think about this one.
4. Live life fully...be creative.
5. Creativity is not a way of thinking. It's a way of life.

Action plan

_____
_____
_____
_____
_____

Compare and despair

1. Your posture gives away your view of yourself. Stand up straight.
2. Only compare yourself to yourself, never, ever, to someone else. If you must compare, at all.
3. Spend time with boosters, not with "derailers. "
4. What you think counts. What they think doesn't.
5. Decide. Decide what? Decide to like yourself. That's all that matters.

Action plan

_____

_____

_____

_____

_____

Spring Cleaning anytime

1. Time to enjoy some fresh air in your life - start with getting rid of those cobwebs to help you appreciate the beauty in life that's been hidden
2. In order to advance, move forward, find increase, you'll need to clear up a couple of things - what are they? Make a list.
3. The clutter between your ears and behind your eyes needs a Spring Cleaning, yes in November. You do want to enjoy the upcoming holidays, right?
4. Your attitude, uhm, can we talk? It needs some freshening up. Trust your gut - it'll tell you where to start.
5. Sure you don't have energy. All that physical, emotional and mental stuff is zapping it. What actions do you need to take to feel renewed? Trust your gut - it'll tell you where to start.

Action plan

_____

_____

_____

_____

_____

Are you a character?

1. Forget your reputation. Johnny Wooden coaches to focus instead on your character.
2. What's character? That's what you reveal about yourself in how you treat people who can do nothing for you.
3. If you saw your character in the mirror instead of your face, how would you really feel?
4. If "opportunity" controls your loyalty, better check your character.
5. You know how you act on your worst days? That's your character showing.

Action plan

_____

_____

_____

_____

_____

Tolerance

1. Want to see the world through a healthier lens? Sensitive souls do.
2. Sensitive folks have big hearts and don't hide them...why ever apologize for being sensitive to others? Don't. Ever.
3. What's with the intolerance in the world that's steadily growing worse? What we should not tolerate is insensitivity.
4. People seem more sensitive to their pets than they are to their neighbors...wtf???
5. How about trying kindness—with no thank you expected? A simple helping, sensitive hand. Imagine that.

Action plan

Smart or wise?

1. Are you a) smart or b) wise? Depends on whether a) you give smart answers or b) ask smart questions.
2. Smart people know what to say. Wise people know when to say it.
3. Wise people are smart enough to know when to walk away from bullsh#$.
4. Ever notice that wise people know what to overlook?
5. The best way I know of being wise, is to be happy.

Action plan

_____

_____

_____

_____

_____

Be active...

1. Healthy is the new fit.
2. Activity leads to optimal health. Did I say exercise leads to fitness? No. I said activity leads to optimal health.
3. Inactivity, more than aging, is harmful.
4. Physical activity sharpens your brain. Before you forget to be active, get moving.
5. Be active, not too much, everyday.

Action plan

_____

_____

_____

_____

_____

Choices

1. Choose: safety or convenience?
2. Safety is expensive? No it's not. It's priceless.
3. Put your safety first...so you can last.
4. If your safety isn't a way of life for you, then safety is just a slogan.
5. You think safety is a joke? Watch out for the punchline. It could be death.

Action plan

_____

_____

_____

_____

_____

What's the matter?

1. You know what really matters? Allow time to show you. It always will.
2. Who matters, who doesn't and who will. That's what life teaches. Learn well.
3. What matters is what you think. Not someone else's opinion or judgment of you.
4. What matters? Much less than you might think.
5. The only time that matters is now. Not then. Now. Stay present and enjoy what matters most.

Action plan

_____

_____

_____

_____

_____

MUSTerbating too much?

1. Be who you are. Who says anyone else MUST approve? It may be nice, but stop MUSTerbating over it. Unhook yourself.
2. If they don't like you, who the _ _ _ _ really cares? How's it going to change your life? Only YOU can do that.
3. You can't stop them from stabbing you in the back or talking about you behind your back. You can only not give a _ _ _ _. Advance in your life in spite of them.
4. Attached to an outcome? Uh oh. Watch out. You're setting yourself up to suffer and feel misery. Detach. Unhook. Smile,
5. Isn't it amazing how much better you feel and do, when you say, and genuinely mean, "So what?"

Action plan

_____

_____

_____

_____

_____

Inspiration

1. Focus more on inspiring and lifting others than your own accomplishments.
2. To be inspired is great. To inspire others is way beyond great.
3. Greatest feedback you can receive? "Wow you inspired me!"
4. When you help others help others, when you feel inspired to inspire others, you're fully alive.
5. Be someone special who helps others feel like someone special. Each of us is, right?

Action plan

_____

_____

_____

_____

_____

Trying to understand them?

1. Trying to understand those who preach love, then hate those who don't love.
2. Trying to understand those who preach encouragement, then complain about those who aren't encouraging.
3. Trying to understand those who preach smiling, and then frown at those who don't smile.
4. Trying to understand those who preach believing, but doubt those who don't believe the way they do.
5. Trying to understand those who preach non-judgment, then judge those who are judgmental.

Action plan

_____
_____
_____
_____
_____

Sensible thinking

1. All I can ever do is simply the best I can do...nothing more is required of me, ever.
2. The path to success, whatever it is for me, includes stumbling, even failing, and always getting back up.
3. I am far more equipped than I believe I am.
4. It's just a hassle, not a horror. It's uncomfortable, not horrible. I can handle it.
5. There is no room for blame in my thinking, ever. Never. I'm the one, the only one, who can turn my life to the positive.

Action plan

_____

_____

_____

_____

_____

Hype, glorious hype

1. Know people who aren't all that they post to be?
2. Believe your own hype and you've started your own destruction.
3. Be wise: remove yourself from any hype that comes your way.
4. Hype your product/service but don't expect to build a long-term business on it. Hype is short term bs.
5. If you've got quality, you have no need for hype.

Action plan

_____

_____

_____

_____

_____

Fear or faith?

1. Which fear do you adhere to?
   Forget everything and run OR
   Face everything and rise.
2. Are you feeding your fear or freeing yourself from it?
3. What's bigger? Your fear or your faith?
4. Are you living your fears? Could be that's why you aren't living your dreams.
5. Ok, so you know that you, and you alone, write the story of your fears...at a huge cost to you -- your self-designed fears are idea crushing, success stalling and experience limiting.

Action plan

_____

_____

_____

_____

_____

Wishing

1. What's wrong with wishing? Sometimes they do come true.
2. W.I.S.H = What I sincerely hope
3. A life filled with more present satisfaction than future wishes is a healthier one.
4. More future wishes and fewer past wishes. More hope, less regret.
5. Live to reduce wishing by increasing satisfaction.

Action plan

_____

_____

_____

_____

_____

Stuck?

1. Want to protect your heart from breaking? Learn to bend. You have spring-back-ability.
2. The stronger and more resilient you grow, the more you'll see that what happens in life can't hurt you.
3. Stop telling yourself those "rut stories" and begin telling yourself "river stories" and your spirit will bend, twist, and never break.
4. When you're resilient, you'll be the one — not others or life -- who chooses what you become.
5. Resilient people enjoy rolling with disruption…we absorb the energy and it fuels us forward always with a smile

Action plan

_____
_____
_____
_____
_____

Getting unstuck

1. Ever notice that resilient people never lose? Never. Ever. Nope, we either win or learn. Always.
2. Always ask, "What's the solution?" Never, ever, get stuck in the rut of, "Oh no, we're finished!"
3. Just when you thought your greatest ally was your greatest ally, you learn that your greatest ally is your resilience.
4. With trillions and trillions of people in the world, why ever bother yourself with what one of them do? Resilient folks don't. Ever. Never.
5. Forget perfect. Shoot for resilient. That builds fearlessness.

Action plan

_____
_____
_____
_____
_____

Freeing yourself

1. Free your mind from worrying - have more trust
2. Live more simply - don't make it all so complicated with "what ifs"
3. Stop being so serious - laugh much more than you do like you did as a child
4. Accept where you are in life - make the most you can of every day
5. Give more and expect less - listen to your heart, it'll tell you when

Action plan

_____
_____
_____
_____
_____

Thoughts to consider

1. Ever notice how the advice some tell others is just the advice they need to follow...but don't?
2. Here's a choice to consider: practice what you preach, or change your speech.
3. Here's another thought to consider: examine yourself very carefully, very, before even thinking of judging others who sin differently than you do.
4. Ever notice that hypocrites are always right?
5. Ya gotta love those holier-than-thou fakes who preach tolerance and "Let's all get along," who are intolerant and hateful when others don't agree with everything they say.

Action plan

_____

_____

_____

_____

_____

Relax

1. Shrink down those blown out of proportion "what if" thoughts
2. There's no way you "should" feel this, or any, time of the year
3. Focus on being present...best present to give? The present
4. Put Zzzzzz on top of your to-do list. The rest of the list? Faggedabowdit
5. Focus your GPS system on Gratitude, Positivity & Sensitivity

Action plan

_____

_____

_____

_____

_____

Problem solving 101

1. Think of challenges as growth opportunities
2. Reward problem-solving and solution-minded thinking
3. Enthusiastically paint an inspirational picture of your vision and articulate the steps to reach the team's goals
4. Show your team how you genuinely care for each individual
5. Demonstrate your self-awareness and acknowledge skills you need to develop

Action plan

_____

_____

_____

_____

_____

Motivating questions

1. What's your favorite way of getting in your own way?
2. If you could change ONLY ONE thing in your life what would that be?
3. What do you stand for?
4. What 3 things could you do today, this coming week, that would leave you feeling really good?
5. What part of yourself are you really dying to let out? What fear story do you tell yourself to stop it from happening?

Action plan

_____

_____

_____

_____

_____

Questions to advance you

1. What do you think your day would be like if you, yes you, really were the reason today that someone smiled?
2. What do you think your day would be like if you, yes you, totally focused on your wellbeing throughout today?
3. What do you think your day would be like if you, yes you, did everything you could today to promote living a full, long and healthy life?
4. What do you think your day would be like if you, yes you, truly embraced the idea today that your body hears everything your mind says?
5. What do you think your day would be like if you, yes you, did everything today with passion and kindness?

Action plan

_____
_____
_____
_____
_____

Rational thinking

1. Sure you follow your heart, but are you careful to bring your brain with you?
2. Rational thinking, rational and emotional thinking, rational and emotional driven behavior—choose rationally.
3. You don't really think your happiness depends on what you have, do you? Rather, it all depends on the quality of your thoughts. Think carefully.
4. Those thoughts you keep twirling around in your head are what you put on your throne and "idolize." Do you like what you're "worshipping""?
5. So, still hating yourself for what you aren't? Uh, maybe it's time to begin liking yourself for what you are?

Action plan

_____

_____

_____

_____

_____

Singular focus

1. Refuse to allow negative seeds to grow in your mind - yes, you can
2. Steadfastly focus only on the good in your life - yes, it can be done
3. Send out only positive vibes - yes, it can be done
4. Only make choices that you won't regret later - yes, it can be done
5. See beyond yourself to create real peace of mind - yes, it can be done

Action plan

_____

_____

_____

_____

_____

Happiness

1. The six words to happier living: "Learn to feel comfortable with uncertainty."
2. Want to feel happier? Free your heart from hate.
3. Is happiness your goal? Let situations in your life be what they are, instead of what you think they should be.
4. Here's your path to happiness as easy as 1, 2, 3 Ready? 1) express gratitude out loud 2) demonstrate kindness publicly 3) savor joy outwardly
5. Forget lowering your expectations - that's bush league. Instead, practice "What a hassle," not "That's a horror," when those expectations don't become reality

Action plan

_____

_____

_____

_____

_____

Likeability

1. Likeable? Make yourself approachable and connect easily.
2. Arrogance will destroy your likeability.
3. Positivity turbocharges likeability. Can't be positive? Be quiet.
4. Never, ever, toot your own horn. Share your substance, not your self-importance.
5. Take delight in the accomplishments of others. Build them up and always acknowledge them.

Action plan

Are you...?

1. Are you running from things that aren't really after you, except in your own mind?
2. Are you insulting yourself by comparing yourself to other people?
3. Are you letting someone else's happiness become more important than your own?
4. Are you spitting your words out before you taste them?
5. Are you still deluding yourself into believing that your success matters more than your significance?

Action plan

_____

_____

_____

_____

_____

Give this

1. Give forgiveness
2. Give authenticity
3. Give the benefit of the doubt
4. Give unlimited thinking
5. Give comfort

Action plan

_____

_____

_____

_____

_____

What do you want?

1. Not going after what you want and wondering why you don't have it?
2. Afraid to ask and wondering why the answer is always "no"?
3. Your thoughts talking you out of stepping forward and wondering why you are still in the same spot?
4. Not making the circumstances you want and wonder why circumstances never fall right for you?
5. Demanding perfection and wonder why you aren't making progress?

Action plan

_____

_____

_____

_____

_____

Stop these irrational behaviors

1. Stop trying to change others. You can't.
2. Stop trying to always be positive. You can't. Accept life's challenges and grow from them.
3. Stop expecting a straight line to success in life, relationships and your career. It doesn't work that way. Pick up and move forward.
4. Stop thinking you can do it all, that you have all the time in the world, & that you can do it all perfectly. Allow "good enough" in the 24 hrs/day you have.
5. Stop trying to control all circumstances. You can't. You can barely control your own thoughts and responses to situations to create your happiness.

Action plan

_____

_____

_____

_____

_____

Stop creating tension

1. Take vacation time and don't forget to turn off your cell phone including the buzz, especially when you sleep.
2. Don't create stress for yourself (it's the only way stress can happen).
3. Help others change, sensitively, wisely and generously.
4. Don't squander your power, authority and talents.
5. Don't talk yourself out of advancement.

Action plan

_____

_____

_____

_____

_____

Hello goodbye

1. New start or a painful finish? What'll you focus on?
2. Starting over or giving up? What'll you call it?
3. Terrific start or hit rock bottom? What'll you think of it?
4. Afraid to say goodbye to the old but still want to say hello to the new? Think that'll work?
5. Think that just because something good ends that nothing better can start? Don't believe everything you think.

Action plan

_____

_____

_____

_____

_____

Judging others?

1. When you judge another you reveal you, not the person you're judging
2. How about being informed, instead of being opinionated?
3. Doesn't it make you feel better about your insecurities when you judge others? Think again.
4. Imagine how much better life would be if you learned, loved and lived...kindness?
5. The opinion of others is not your reality-they just feel superior because you sin differently than they do...care less, live happier.

Action plan

_____
_____
_____
_____
_____

More on success

1. Looking for success? Build happiness in whatever you do.
2. If your self-image isn't strong and positive, neither will be your success.
3. Success is a more or less game. Promise less, deliver more.
4. Imagine your bank account growing and you don't. Think that's success? Wrong.
5. Rich people have money. Wealthy people have time. Wise people are grateful for whatever they have.

Action plan

_____
_____
_____
_____
_____

C'mon, really

1. C'mon, you know the best project you can work on is yourself. Right!
2. C'mon, you know if you want to be positive it'll sure help to hang out with positive people.
3. C'mon, try leading with your heart to see how well things fall into place.
4. C'mon, you know it's what you do that's the difference between where and who you are and where and who you want to be.
5. C'mon, you know that if you don't control your mind, others will.

Action plan

_____

_____

_____

_____

_____

Extending the quality of your life

1. Make time to deeply and compassionately value yourself
2. Delete the pills and alcohol to avoid inevitable long-term life-shortening consequences
3. Bring gratitude, positivity and positive people into your life
4. Stop "reducing" and "managing" stress! Instead, learn how to prevent stress in the first place. It's not inevitable. It's in your thinking.
5. Shhh. That means give yourself a chance to hear your deepest thoughts. How? Mindfulness is the best way.

Action plan

_____

_____

_____

_____

_____

Letting it go

1. Own your self-worth...never give another's opinion of you the ability to determine anything about you
2. Pick your battles wisely, forgive those who truly harm you to allow yourself to advance, yet don't give them a second chance to do it again
3. Where are you focused? On the past? On your problems? Don't let your past errors be your present reality. Your misfortunes can be your fortunes when you focus on learning and solutions
4. Let go...of negativity, of negative people, of grudges, of thoughts that create stress
5. Learn to say "no" comfortably with no excuses, "I don't want to" sounds more honest than "Oh I'm sorry I can't"

Action plan

_____

_____

_____

_____

_____

Win or l___ ?

1. Winners come back, no matter what the results were last week.
2. Oh no, I'm so sorry you've got that scar! Stop complaining!! - That just means that your wound has healed.
3. While many are busy making excuses, the savvy ones are busy making millions.
4. Why do so many constantly feel a need to compete? Look at the mega-successful - they don't compete. They only dominate.
5. People you don't even know hate you? Congratulations. You must be among the best!! Win or learn…never lose.

Action plan

_____

_____

_____

_____

_____

What's stopping you?

1. Stumble over something in the road? What in your thinking is stopping you from using it as a stepping-stone to achievement?
2. Walt Disney was fired from his first newspaper job because he "wasn't creative or imaginative." Imagine if he let that label stick on him. What harmful label are you going to shrug off today?
3. Secrets of achievement? Strive to be a good person, one who lives a decent and honorable life.
4. Oh you want more secrets of achievement? Be radically kind-hearted and tell the truth.
5. What?? You really want more secrets of achievement? Always do what's right and only see the good along the road of your life.

Action plan

_____
_____
_____
_____
_____

When your work culture is all wrong

1. Employees can't do their best work
2. Top-tier talent leaving due to ill culture, lack of progress
3. Not everyone included in organizational design
4. Innovation stalled, becoming less competitive
5. Organizational structure favors some and not all staff

Action plan

_____
_____
_____
_____
_____

THINking right

1. It's entirely an inside job--change your *THIN*king first if you genuinely want to change your body
2. Your success is not at all in your scale, it's entirely in your head
3. Your attitude determines your weight more than anything else
4. Losing weight is not "hard." THINking it is though, will put on pounds
5. Food is an important part of your weight loss success. However, what you THINk about food is far more important.

Action plan

_____

_____

_____

_____

_____

Fitness madness

1. Ooh, "I don't sweat, I sparkle." Uhm, no you sweat
2. Ooh, "Unless you puke, faint or die, keep going." Uhm, are you really that stupid?
3. Ooh, "Sweat is fat crying." Uhm, uh fat doesn't cry.
4. Ooh, "Strong is the new skinny." Uhm, not.
5. Ooh, "I wear black to the gym because exercise is a funeral for my fat." Uhm, no, actually exercise is just good for your overall health...nothing to do with funerals except postponing your own

Action plan

_____
_____
_____
_____
_____

Destined to ruin your happiness

1. Comparison & self-criticism
2. Lack of gratitude
3. Fear, blame & anger
4. Dwelling on your yesterdays and/or your tomorrows
5. Demanding and trying to control, what's not in your control

Action plan

_____

_____

_____

_____

_____

Your children are watching

1. What do you want your children to remember about you?
2. Do you know who your children's role models are? Are these the kind of role models you would choose for them?
3. When you freak out about something that went wrong, a scratch on your new car, a spill on the white sofa, a stain on your dress, what are you teaching your children is most important in life?
4. What are your praises you want your children to mention in their eulogy of you?
5. What can you do to insure that your children will have something good to say about you?

Action plan

_____
_____
_____
_____
_____

Awareness

1. The first step for any transformational, sustainable change is *awareness*.
2. Be aware that what you put after, "I am _____," will shape your reality.
3. Awareness means observing a moment, accepting it, not judging it. Now you're ready to savor deep, authentic self-insight.
4. Acting without awareness can be seriously harmful for your well-being. It means your choices will be quite restricted.
5. If you have awareness, kindness and gratitude, what else would you need to live a happy, satisfied life of wellbeing?

Action plan

_____

_____

_____

_____

_____

Living better 101

1. Rephrase your goals so that they are entirely within your control
2. Hold on to nothing you are not fully prepared to lose
3. Live more simply - resist materialism
4. Accept what you cannot change - practice misfortune
5. Live in accordance with nature - refuse to consider yourself a victim

Action plan

_____
_____
_____
_____
_____

Attitude

1. Your attitude is like a flat tire. To go anywhere, you'll have to change it.
2. The right attitude towards insults is to understand that you first have to value the other person's opinion before the insult matters.
3. Your attitude - and only your attitude - is the difference between a good day and a bad day.
4. You know that your attitude is entirely your decision, right? It depends on nobody else.
5. Take the attitude that what you do makes a difference. It sure does.

Action plan

_____
_____
_____
_____
_____

Is your team winning?

1. How do you know you're on a winning team? You all fully trust each other.
2. How do you know you're on a winning team? You all fully respect each other.
3. How do you know you're on a winning team? You all fully understand each other.
4. How do you know you're on a winning team? You all fully enjoy each other.
5. How do you know you're on a winning team? You all support, help and enjoy each other.

Action plan

_____

_____

_____

_____

_____

Open minded?

1. Open minded? Isn't it nice to be free of illusions?
2. Open minded? Isn't it nice not caring if you're right, and instead caring to understand?
3. Closed minded? What's it like missing so much of life?
4. Closed minded? What's it like only hearing what you want to hear?
5. The healthy mind is wide open. The closed mind's mouth is usually what's wide open.

Action plan

_____
_____
_____
_____
_____

Getting along superbly

1. Observe no unfriendliness in others
2. Stop gossiping about others
3. Communicate friendliness in your eyes, body, language, tone of voice and words you use
4. Connect with the interests, wants and needs of others
5. Don't jump to negative conclusions or judgmental assumptions

Action plan

_____
_____
_____
_____
_____

Deeper thoughts

1. Can you view the insulting words of another as "just words"? Use their shoddy behavior to learn to speak with others in kind and respectful ways.
2. Remember that no matter where you mind is, you are always in the present. That's where your power to self-correct lies, in the now.
3. Sages ask, "Who is an honorable person?" They answer, "The one who shows honor and respect to others." Do you?
4. Your facial expression gives it all away. The only way for your expression to fully change is for you to change your inner thoughts about another. Don't, and see how your conscious mind won't control all of your facial muscles.
5. Inner calm will help you speak with others in a calm way, promoting harmony between you and others.

Action plan

_____

_____

_____

_____

_____

Why create problems?

1. Your thinking creates problems that aren't real
2. Focusing on problems enlarges and grows them
3. Create more problems by awfulizing, catastrophizing, demanding and rating people...oh yeah, and can't stand it itis
4. Irrational beliefs about negative events create problems while rational beliefs about the same events don't
5. You'll create plenty of problems believing that you must do well, others must treat you well and life must be easy

Action plan

_____
_____
_____
_____
_____

Healing

---

1. Your own healing is a genuine gift to the healing of others
2. Before you heal, you need to recognize you're wounded
3. Your soul knows what you need to heal. Be mindful enough - present, non-judgmental & aware - to listen
4. Healed pain is the foundation of all wisdom
5. When the damage no longer controls your life, you're on the road to genuine healing

Action plan

Technology got you down?

1. Less emphasis on financial targets and more on life goals
2. Watch for increasing automation while increasing meaningful, emotional personal touch
3. Get beyond your material zone and shift into your experience zone
4. Share more of your genuine self, connect more personally with others, in a transformational way -technologically. Embrace it.
5. Speaking of embracing, are you fully ready for robotics and AI? Resist at your own peril. It's changing everything in fitness, health, wellness, business and education.

Action plan

_____
_____
_____
_____
_____

Mindfulness will...

1. Mindfulness will promote your superior work output
2. Mindfulness will promote your innovative thinking
3. Mindfulness will promote your attractiveness
4. Mindfulness will promote your authenticity
5. Mindfulness will promote your trustworthiness

Action plan

_____
_____
_____
_____
_____

People...sigh

1. There'll always be people who want to see you do well, just not better than them
2. Don't ever let jealous people control your dreams or limit your spirit
3. If you don't set limits on your giving, takers will keep taking
4. People feel jealous because they think you are a threat, they want to be you or they hate themselves
5. Gratitude for genuine, not fake, good is a magnet for miracles

Action plan

_____
_____
_____
_____
_____

Moving on 101

1. Don't ever let perfection impede your advancement and joy
2. Embrace every change that comes your way, with curiosity and gratitude for what it'll bring for you
3. Recognize that all motivation is self-motivation. Nobody ever really motivates you. Only you do
4. Live now, not through the rear view mirror.
5. Never ever take offense. Why bother? Give another that power over you? Not ever

Action plan

_____
_____
_____
_____
_____

Recovery

1. Let your burdens go and face the day with faith that everything gets better.
2. The most important person in your recovery...yep, it's you.
3. Recovery requires retiring...your irrational inner, lying, disordering voice.
4. Recovery may "seem" scary, but isn't staying the same scarier? Progress means struggle.
5. When you fall on your face, your soul is cheering for you to get up and keep moving forward.

Action plan

_____

_____

_____

_____

_____

What's your choice?

1. Wouldn't you prefer honesty over sugar coated bullshit?
2. You may not get a whole lot of friend being honest, but you'll sure get the right ones
3. Rather be impressive than honest? Pffff, just keep walking.
4. Proverbs teaches, "The first step towards greatness is to be honest"
5. Want to be trusted? Tell, speak, live and love honesty.

Action plan

_____
_____
_____
_____
_____

Chill will ya?

1. Life is really so much easier when you just chill out.
2. What's chilling? Doing nothing and not being bored.
3. Keep calm and trust. That'll help you chill.
4. Telling someone who's upset to chill out, won't work.
5. No time to chill? That means only one thing. You definitely need to chill. Now.

Action plan

_____

_____

_____

_____

_____

Creating victimhood

1. Ok look, if you keep inflating the good of the past, see the present worse it really is, and worry that the future will be bad, no wonder you aren't happy.
2. Everything you're running away from is in your head.
3. You're a victim all right, a victim of your own thinking.
4. Convince your mind you can stand it and your body will listen.
5. If your mind is full of fear, there's not much room for dreams.

Action plan

_____

_____

_____

_____

_____

Stress is your creation - entirely

1. A major cause of stress is whining, demanding and insisting that life is not the way you think it must be — and believing it's horrible, terrible and awful.
2. Stress is grounded in self-defeating assumptions. For example, the dark doesn't stress you out — it's what you believe is IN the dark.
3. You never "get stressed out." You always create and contribute to your own stress.
4. Instead of avoiding changing your own attitudes about conditions you believe are frustrating, if stress is a big part of your life, you've probably only tried to change the conditions themselves or run away from them.
5. Stress can be entirely prevented by correcting your faulty conceptions, self-signals, erroneous beliefs and choosing one thought over another. Oh yeah, physical activity, nature, positive friends, restorative sleep, healthy nutrition, and faith will also help.

Action plan

_____

_____

_____

_____

_____

Work-life balance isn't!

1. Forget work-life balance…it's all about making a life, not a living.
2. Think of it like this - when you take time for your life, you'll have more inspiration to work.
3. Work-life balance is easier than you think - make more life withdrawals than life deposits in your life and you'll be out of balance.
4. When work is a pleasure and life is a joy, you won't have to think about work-life balance.
5. Work, family, community and self - pursue excellence in each of these areas simultaneously and you'll be stronger in each one AND all will benefit. Sounds like great balance to me.

Action plan

_____

_____

_____

_____

_____

Love

1. Watch out how you speak to yourself. Remember, you are listening and you may be lessened by what you hear.
2. Searching for love? Be sure - really be certain - you love yourself first.
3. Are you proud of the space you take up in this world? If you aren't then why would you demand anyone else to be proud of you?
4. You can't find self-worth, self-respect or self-love anywhere else but...inside of yourself.
5. The more you approve of yourself, the happier you'll be and the less you'll need others to approve of you. Because you'll never really be happy if you constantly demand others approve of you.

Action plan

Forget perfection

1. Light bulb burned out the other day. Guess what? Didn't buy a new home. Just a new light bulb. It's not ever all or nothing It's imperfect.
2. I gave up perfection long ago. Excellence, grace, progress and being real are different. Those I"ll never give up.
3. What's with people? Fearing rejection, wanting attention, craving affection and dreaming of perfection.
4. Instead of "perfect" beauty, how about confidence, character and charisma? Aren't they achievable beauty?
5. Notice how to spell "imperfect"? That'd be "I'm perfect." Hmmm, could it be that perfect is really being imperfect?

Action plan

_____

_____

_____

_____

_____

Grow up!

1. How about using your words for integrity, truth and love, not gossip? Grow up!
2. How about not making everything so personal? It isn't always about you. Grow up!
3. How about being immune to the opinions of others to avoid reacting like a victim all of the time? Grow up!
4. How about communicating with others clearly to avoid drama and misunderstanding? Grow up!
5. How about just doing your best and not focusing on anyone else? Grow up!

Action plan

_____

_____

_____

_____

_____

Fear

1. Count the words *"Do not be afraid"* in the Bible. I counted 365. Hmm, could be a daily reminder, huh?
2. It takes overcoming self-talk of fear to become extraordinary and who you want to be. Worth it, don't you think?
3. The less you fear, that dangerous illusion/prediction of awful, terrible and horrible outcomes, the more you succeed in life.
4. I bet that every excuse you have ever had is grounded in lack of self-confidence…that is fear. Practice being fearless and see how much more you tackle.
5. Fearlessness = limitlessness.

Action plan

_____

_____

_____

_____

_____

Of course!

1. Of course happiness is an inside job. Joy just does not ever exist out in the world.
2. Of course claiming your power is an inside job. Strength just does not ever exist out in the world.
3. Of course well-being is an inside job. Health just does not ever exist out in the world.
4. Of course motivation is an inside job. Achievement just does not ever exist out in the world.
5. Of course positivity is an inside job. Confidence just does not ever exist out in the world.

Action plan

_____
_____
_____
_____
_____

It's all in your power

1. Never let the world blow out your candle. Your inner strength will always prevent that.
2. Whatever you need to make yourself happy lies inside of you. It's your inner strength.
3. When you bring your inner strength out, you can achieve remarkable heights.
4. Stumble over an obstacle on the outside? Get up on the inside and you'll still come out on top.
5. Want to build your inner strength? Try compassion...for others and for yourself.

Action plan

_____

_____

_____

_____

_____

Who's your tribe?

1. Amazing people don't just become amazing alone
2. We all need someone who inspires us, guides our growth, channels our energy, and promotes our goals.
3. A great mentor helps you see the beauty of your dreams.
4. Great mentors are more interested in your success than in the success of your business.
5. You know you've got a great mentor if he/she is hard to part with and impossible to forget.

Action plan

_____
_____
_____
_____
_____

Improving?

1. Here's an idea-be so busy improving yourself you have zero time to criticize others.
2. Never pass up a chance to improve yourself.
3. Notice what "Improve" starts with?
4. Self-improvement starts with believing you are a work in progress, not a finished product.
5. No bullshit, transformational self-improvement requires that you fully accept that your problems are your own and not anyone else's fault, and that only you control your on destiny.

Action plan

_____

_____

_____

_____

_____

Make believe

1. Remember when you played make believe and it was just like real? Play make believe now.
2. Isn't it just really all make believe? Play make believe now.
3. Make believe that you believe that you'll make it, and you will. Play make believe now.
4. Making believe means changing your thinking. It works. Play make believe now.
5. Happiness is watching your kids play make believe. Play make believe now with them.

Action plan

_____
_____
_____
_____
_____

Who says?

1. Who says you "must" worry about unpleasant or dangerous things happening?
2. WS you "must" be perfect, a success & not make mistakes?
3. WS you "must" have approval & avoid all disapproval?
4. WS you "must" have things your way otherwise it's intolerable?
5. WS you "must" not feel discomfort or pain & avoid them at all costs?

Action plan

_____

_____

_____

_____

_____

Success

1. Real success is not tied to a time limit. You'll achieve it when you achieve it.
2. Bring your passion and your career into alignment and you'll see the success you imagined.
3. Success begins in your mind. Be sure you are not talking yourself out of the success you want.
4. Success is truly yours for the taking. Take it.
5. Sometimes the best career moves are not the ones you planned for, but were the ones you were open to.

Action plan

_____

_____

_____

_____

_____

Kindness

1. Who really needs a reason to be kind to anyone?
2. Kindness is the best religion to follow.
3. Looking for a really special gift? Give kindness - not only will it lift someone else, but it'll lift you too.
4. More & less. Guess which? Kindness, hurry, laughter or worry.
5. When you give with authentic kindness, you don't count the cost.

Action plan

_____

_____

_____

_____

_____

What do you see in the mirror?

1. I'd love to see the look that some would have if they saw their character instead of their face when they look in the mirror.
2. "Mirror, mirror, on the wall, who is the most self-righteous of them all?"
3. Sometimes the most authentic people are covered in tattoos while the most negatively judgmental gossipers are found leading religious institutions.
4. You can be an ass without being self-righteous, but you can't be self-righteous without being an ass.
5. Moral indignation won't make you a saint. It'll make you holier than thou

Action plan

_____
_____
_____
_____
_____

A day off – savor it

1. It's a day off so slow down. C'mon, really. Savor the moments of this beautiful day.
2. Moments, not days, are what we recall. Savor each with wide-eyed awareness.
3. Raise your standard and savor your new experience.
4. See the happiness in front of you? No? Turn your awareness button on and savor the joy.
5. The best moments come with a price. The price is to savor & enjoy them.

Action plan

_____

_____

_____

_____

_____

Vacation or vocation?

1. I've always made my vocation my vacation. But this coming week, I won't even know what day of the week it is.
2. Nothing to do. All week to do it. Ahhhh.
3. Watching the world going to work. Ahhhh, now that's a vacation.
4. Good family vacations aren't designed to escape daily life. We create our family vacations to make sure that life doesn't escape us.
5. Notice how a family vacation means that the family goes away for a rest…along with grandparents who see to it that everyone gets it.

Action plan

_____
_____
_____
_____
_____

Facebooking your problems?

1. Here's some good advice. Face your problems. "Don't Facebook your problems."
2. Notice how Facebook is like a refrigerator? Yeah, you know, when you are bored, you keep it open. And you keep checking it and there's nothing good in it.
3. Ever consider that Facebook is like being in jail? Yeah, you know, you sit around and waste time, write on walls and get poked by strangers.
4. Being popular on Facebook is like sitting at the cool table at a mental hospital - it's the only place you can talk to a wall and not look like a complete psycho.
5. I love it when someone actually whines, hurt and indignant, "And you even UNFRIENDED me on Facebook!" OMG Facebook needs an "I don't want to hear your drama" button. I'd still unfriend :-)

Action plan

_____
_____
_____
_____
_____

Talk to yourself ...

1. Talk to yourself and finish this: positively "At least I'm_____."
2. Talk to yourself and finish this positively: "Who'd have thought I _____."
3. Talk to yourself and finish this positively: "I am_____."
4. Talk to yourself like you would talk with someone you love - otherwise you are giving up on self-esteem.
5. Talk to yourself and say, "I can' imagine anything better than being me."

Action plan

_____

_____

_____

_____

_____

Whine, whine, whine

1. Why are you whining? Don't like the way the table's set? Turn it over.
2. Inferior intellects, inferior self-esteem…the substance of whiners.
3. Stop whining about things you aren't willing to change.
4. When people whine about not having the time to do something, remind them that they have the time to whine.
5. While you whine about faults you find, others are busy finding solutions.

Action plan

_____

_____

_____

_____

_____

Who's in charge of your feelings?

1. Yes, the world is full of suffering. But have you noticed that it's also full of surmounting?
2. Do you realize—really realize —that ALL of your emotions originate solely in your thinking? What the heck are you busy blaming anyone else for?
3. You'll never fully be free until you no longer ruminate over things you can't control — like most things in your life.
4. Everyone has illusions that they believe are the "Truth." But dogmatic thinking, demanding/insisting/expecting (D.I.E.) is the greatest obstacle to being happy.
5. You know who your real boss is? It's that mental attitude that you cling to.

Action plan

_____
_____
_____
_____
_____

The best GPS system

1. Never, ever, frighten yourself about change. Welcome it. You'll never find success without forward movement.
2. Forget perfect. Remember what you learned from every misstep.
3. Curiosity may have killed the cat, but it fuels your success. Questions open new doors, paths, and possibilities.
4. Be guided by my personal GPS system — gratitude, positivity, and sensitivity. That'll lead you, always, to feeling good about your life, and that's success.
5. Success is anchored in your taking care of yourself — thinking well, feeling well, eating well, moving well, sleeping well and living well.

Action plan

_____
_____
_____
_____
_____

Please remember

1. Please remember that every person has pride and dignity - even if just a little. Be mindful of everyone.
2. Please remember you've made plenty of mistakes, so don't overly compliment yourself.
3. Please remember you don't know enough to judge others.
4. Please remember to cheer for others and practice kindness.
5. Please remember how easily it is for you to become pessimistic, angry and negative. These emotions limit you ability to move forward.

Action plan

_____

_____

_____

_____

_____

5 rules

1. Smile more — a lot more.
2. Live simply — a lot more simply
3. Worry less — a whole lot less
4. Let go — of whatever you are dragging around that's dragging you down
5. Never blame — you are the reason and the only reason for your unhappiness

Action plan

_____

_____

_____

_____

_____

Your focus is your choice

1. Don't go out without your pants on — wear your positive pants, that is.
2. Isn't it amazing how that beautiful destination you've arrived at required you to go through all of those scary turns and potholes in the road?
3. Why focus on problems when you can focus on joys in life?
4. What happens in life and what you feel are never linked. Only your thinking links them…the link is what you think.
5. Nobody can ever dull your shine — only your thoughts do that.

Action plan

_____
_____
_____
_____
_____

Want to?

1. Wishing for a rose? First, respect the thorns
2. Want to grasp it all? First be ready to lose it all
3. Want to sleep till noon? First get a reputation as an early riser
4. Want to be a giant? First remember it won't happen by hanging out with dwarfs
5. Want to free your mind of sorrowful thoughts? First don't be afraid of crying

Action plan

_____
_____
_____
_____
_____

Watch how you transform

1. Forget your age and live your life, and watch how you transform yourself
2. Treat information like oxygen, and watch how you transform yourself
3. Grow your focus and awareness, and watch how you transform yourself
4. Think much bigger than you've been doing, and watch how you transform yourself
5. Here's the big one: talk more nicely to yourself about yourself, and watch how you transform yourself

Action plan

_____

_____

_____

_____

_____

Education

1. The one thing you'll never lose is your education
2. Educating your brain without your heart is not education
3. My education didn't prepare me for life...it is my life
4. Forget what you learned in school? That's your education you're left with
5. If you learned how to think, not what to think, you had a fine education

Action plan

_____

_____

_____

_____

Sunshine

1. How will you create your own sunshine today?
2. How will you be someone's sunshine today?
3. How will you keep telling yourself that the sun will shine on you today?
4. How will you look at the brighter side of life today?
5. How will you enjoy the sunshine? By weathering a storm first.

Action plan

_____
_____
_____
_____
_____

Professional?

1. If you think it's expensive to hire a professional, wait until you hire an amateur
2. What kind of profession is based on someone reading a book and passing an online multiple choice quiz?
3. Ever notice that those who appear the holiest are often the most judgmental?
4. Accept the apology you wanted, but never got...it makes life so much more enjoyable.
5. Watch out for the takers, the fakers and the makers.

Action plan

_____

_____

_____

_____

_____

Fame or success

1. Who seriously confuses fame with success? Don't.
2. Remember "everyone will be famous for 15 minutes"? Have you had your 15 minutes yet? Enjoy it?
3. Fame on Facebook is like being wealthy in Monopoly.
4. Fame or fortune? Fame, or health? Fame, or love? Get it?
5. You can't have fame without gullible people.

Action plan

_____
_____
_____
_____
_____

Tense or relaxed?

1. Tense? That's you thinking about who you "must" be. Relaxed? That's you thinking about you are.
2. Relax. Notice that you have, do and are...enough.
3. When you remain true to what keeps you feeling alive, you feel relaxed, right? Take the hint.
4. Since you, and only you, are in charge of what you feel, what they heck would make you choose to feel anything but relaxed?
5. How many more times do you choose to "be there and do that"? Try a cheerful frame of mind, close your eyes and let your relaxation grow.

Action plan

Moving forward

1. Want to move forward? Can't stay where you are.
2. The past is your lesson. The future is your motivation. The present? That's your gift.
3. Who says you need to have it all clear to move forward?
4. Yesterday ought not take up too much of your time today.
5. Often you need to say goodbye in order for a new hello.

Action plan

_____
_____
_____
_____
_____

Friends or backstabbers?

1. Don't you love it when people show you why they can't be trusted?
2. Ever notice how "best friends" and "backstabber" have the same number of letters? Hmm gotta wonder why, right? Just be sure you know the difference between the two.
3. You do realize, right, that backstabbers are only powerful when your back is turned?
4. Here's what a backstabber really is: a nasty person who picks a nice person who they are jealous of and tries to make everyone else hate them.
5. Yep, scum'll stab you in your back and then blame you for bleeding.

Action plan

_____

_____

_____

_____

_____

When others doubt you

1. Give people more chances than they deserve, but once your done, you are done.
2. When people judge others favorably, they not only help others, but themselves as well.
3. Don't you feel motivated when others doubt you? After all their judgments define them, not you.
4. It's been said to give people three chances: first chance is to give others the benefit of the doubt, second chance is to give yourself the benefit of the doubt and third chance, game's over.
5. Controllers, abusers and manipulators always judge others unfavorably and never themselves. Don't burn bridges with them, instead, consider just loosening the bolts a bit everyday :-)

Action plan

_____
_____
_____
_____
_____

Hurt?

1. Accept what is. Hard to do, I know. But wait. There's more. Let go of what was. Ouch. That may be more difficult. But wait, there's still more. Have faith in what's coming. That oughta be easy, right?
2. Why are you justifying holding on to toxicity? There are lessons in letting go and moving on.
3. It may hurt to let go, but it'll hurt more to hold on.
4. You have no real reason to stay? That'd be a real good reason to go.
5. Letting go of toxic people is an act of self-care, not cruelty. But you'll be blamed regardless. Who cares?

Action plan

_____

_____

_____

_____

_____

What are you choosing?

1. You can either feed your negative or feed your positive. Whichever you feed, wins. Get it?
2. You can believe your own judgments, opinions and perspectives or choose to see the good that lies beyond appearances. Get it?
3. You can either choose to see the beauty that everyone has, or be blind to it. Get it?
4. You can be excited for the good things that are coming, or choose to believe nothing good will come. Get it?
5. You can wake up feeling exceptional, unique and victorious, or you can choose to wake up thinking life sucks. Get it?

Action plan

_____

_____

_____

_____

_____

Unity

1. Remember that unity begins with you. Ohhhh, you thought it meant the other guy? Nope.
2. Want victory? Create unity first. Right?
3. Afraid that you'll have to stay in line to advance unity? Not according to MLK, Jr. "Unity has never meant uniformity."
4. Ever wonder why the loudest voices come from those who advocate divisiveness? What about the rest of us? Where's our voice?
5. Be an encourager...leave the haters to stew in their ugly juices.

Action plan

_____
_____
_____
_____
_____

Feed your fear?

1. You can change the entire concept of what's possible with one daring thought you express
2. Are you feeding your fear or your courage? Share that courage and starve that fear.
3. Ready to let go of the familiar? That's courage.
4. Your greatest growth can come from your biggest fear.
5. Your fear will kill your dreams more than your actual failures.

Action plan

_____
_____
_____
_____
_____

It's a miracle!

1. It'll feel like a miracle when you stop letting people stay in your life longer than they deserve.
2. It'll feel like a miracle when you stop wasting your time on people who only want you around when it fits their needs.
3. It'll feel like a miracle when you realize the people who don't approve of you make your stronger. Say "thank you" to them.
4. It'll feel like a miracle when you realize the only time people don't like gossip is when it's about them.
5. It'll feel like a miracle when you stop wishing that you could just "unmeet" someone.

Action plan

_____
_____
_____
_____
_____

Relax

1. Relax and think about all of the beauty that's around you right now...feel better?
2. Relax and think about this: you do enough, are enough and have enough...feel better?
3. Relax and think about the fact that where you are right now, with all that you have and don't have, you can do so much to help others....feel better?
4. Relax and think about all of the people that have come into your life as blessings...and those who've served as lessons...feel better?
5. Relax and think about how to stop undervaluing what you are and overvaluing what you aren't...feel better?

Action plan

_____

_____

_____

_____

_____

No explanation necessary

1. Your life situation is yours. No explanation necessary.
2. Your priorities are yours. No explanation necessary.
3. Your physical shape and appearance are yours. No explanation necessary.
4. Your career, personal lifestyle, religious and political views, and even your sex life are yours. No explanation necessary.
5. You really aren't sorry and don't agree with what the other person believes? No explanation necessary.

Action plan

_____

_____

_____

_____

_____

Retired?

1. Feeling rested, refreshed, happy, content, invigorated, refocused? Must be retired.
2. Reordered priorities and freely choosing where you devote your time? Must be retired.
3. Don't want to, don't have to and can't be made to? Must be retired.
4. The world feeling sorry that you're retiring? That's the best time to ReWire, ReFire and...ReTire.
5. Living your dream with fun and continued challenging opportunities? Yep, must be retired.

Action plan

_____

_____

_____

_____

_____

Healthy living

1. Make healthy a way of living, not a goal
2. Do you care enough for yourself to live a healthy lifestyle?
3. Whether you write it down or not, your body is keeping an accurate journal.
4. Since you are what you eat, don't eat fake, cheap, fast or easy.
5. You know what giving up feels like, right? Now see what happens if you don't.

Action plan

_____

_____

_____

_____

_____

Taking care of yourself

1. It's your life so don't let others tell you how to live it
2. The depth of your struggle will determine the height of your success
3. Be sure you give yourself the right to have weaknesses
4. Work at needing less and you'll have, and become, more
5. Ever meet astringent person who did not have a hard past? Me neither.

Action plan

_____
_____
_____
_____
_____

Self-confidence

1. Want to boost your self-confidence? Do something you've been fearful of doing.
2. Want to boost your self-confidence? Enjoy your imperfections.
3. Want to boost your self-confidence? Practice thinking, "I'm well able to do what I need."
4. Want to boost your self-confidence? Feed your faith & starve your fear, call in victory, not defeat.
5. Want to boost your self-confidence? Start every morning by calling on your inner cheerleader to insure you won't let anyone steal your joy.

Action plan

_____

_____

_____

_____

_____

Meaning

1. At some point in life, the simple things become more meaningful. When? That'd be right now.
2. Want a meaningful experience? Overcome an interesting challenge.
3. What's more meaningful to you? Your significance, or your success?
4. One of the legs of the tripod of happiness is meaningfulness. What are the other two? Hint: pleasure & engagement. Oops, was that too much of a hint?
5. You're not waiting for life to give you meaning are you? Haha, it's the other way around silly.

Action plan

_____
_____
_____
_____
_____

What's it your business?

1. What they think of you, really, it's none of your business.
2. The only place to look for happiness is in your head.
3. Comparing yourself to others? Could be a source of your despair.
4. Want to smile more? Remember you don't own all of the problems of the world.
5. Still thinking you can control your life? Don't believe everything you think!

Action plan

_____
_____
_____
_____
_____

Ever notice...?

1. Ever notice that wise people aren't always silent but know when to be?
2. Ever notice that wise people no how to walk away from nonsense?
3. Do you make more opportunities than you find? Ever notice that wise people do?
4. Ever notice that a conversation with a wise person can beat a decade of studying?
5. Ever notice that wise people know they're fools while fools think they're wise?

Action plan

_____
_____
_____
_____
_____

Kindness

1. Want to turbocharge your kindness? Focus on those you can help and want your help, not on those who don't want your help or who you can't help.
2. Want to turbocharge your kindness? Just because others are unkind and ungiving has no bearing on you. Continue being kind and giving.
3. Want to turbocharge your kindness? Instead of complaining that others keep asking you to help them, see it as what it is…an enormous compliment.
4. Want to turbocharge your kindness? When negative people complain about you, understand it probably isn't really about you. It's more likely revealing something about them.
5. Want to turbocharge your kindness? Don't believe everything you think…remember that just because something works for you doesn't mean it must, should or ought to work for others.

Action plan

_____
_____
_____
_____
_____

What's faith?

1. Wouldn't it be nice if there were visiting hours in heaven? That's faith.
2. Don't you really believe that better things are coming? That's faith.
3. You know that light that shines through the darkness? That's faith.
4. Spending time with God will put it all in perspective. That's faith.
5. Looking for inner strength and a healthy sense of balance in life? That's faith.

Action plan

_____
_____
_____
_____
_____

Single?

1. Don't label yourself as "single" or "not taken." Instead, see yourself as just waiting for something real.
2. Don't label yourself as "single." Instead, see yourself as being in a long term relationship with fun and adventure.
3. Don't label yourself as "single." Instead, recognize that you're strong enough to enjoy life without depending on others.
4. Don't label yourself as "single" or "not good enough to be with the right person." Instead, see that you're just too good to be with the wrong person.
5. Don't confuse being "single" with "being available." They aren't always equivalent.

Action plan

_____

_____

_____

_____

_____

Pain? Obstacle? Being stopped?

1. Feeling pain today? That's just the strength you'll feel tomorrow.
2. OK, so something you don't like happened. You can define yourself by the event, destroy yourself with the event, derail yourself with it, or strengthen yourself with the event.
3. Facing an obstacle? Say "THANK YOU" since you can strengthen yourself by growing through it, not just going through it.
4. Want to really feel success? Admire the strength in others that you don't have.
5. Remember that even those who stop you...don't stop you. Only you stop you. Why would you? And more, why then blame and complain?

Action plan

_____

_____

_____

_____

_____

Deep thinking

1. Facing a challenge today? Sure it's interesting, right? But over-coming it is what makes the challenge meaningful.
2. You'll spend all week working, right? But what'll you do to make what you do, meaningful? Just doing it isn't enough.
3. It takes being mindful to be meaningful.
4. Are you searching for the easy way or for the meaningful way? There's a very large difference. Search wisely.
5. Being aware of your mortality may help wake you up to mean-ing…if not, uh oh.

Action plan

_____
_____
_____
_____
_____

How are they treating you?

1. Happiness comes more easily without feeling the need for any-one else's approval.
2. When other people treat you poorly, walk away, smile and keep being YOU.
3. Don't ever let someone else's bitterness change the person you are.
4. One of the most freeing things you learn in life is that you don't have to like everyone and everyone doesn't have to like you, and that's OK.
5. Happiness and success is all about spending your life in your own way. Be yourself. No one can ever tell you you're doing it wrong.

Action plan

_____

_____

_____

_____

_____

Increasing peace in your life

1. Do something today that you'll than yourself tomorrow for doing.
2. Tell the next five people you see, "thank you" for something they did, small or large.
3. Sometimes it's even ok to thank your middle finger for sticking up for you.
4. Looking for a peaceful mantra? Try, "Thank you."
5. What breath have you taken throughout your life that you're not thankful for? Want to rethink that one?

Action plan

_____

_____

_____

_____

_____

Success or failure?

1. What's the opposite of success? Failure?? Of course, not. That's part of success.
2. Success going to your head is as bad as failure going to your heart.
3. Failing largely trumps not trying.
4. Don't think of yourself as a failure. Think of yourself as success in the making.
5. You know those small people who want, wish, hope and pray for you to fail? They're your steps tools to success. Thank them for the lift.

Action plan

_____

_____

_____

_____

_____

Ever feel like saying…?

1. Don't you ever feel like saying, "Oops, sorry that the middle of my sentence interrupted the beginning of your sentence"?
2. Don't you ever feel like saying, "OK, we'll make believe that I give a shit and leave it at that"?
3. Don't you ever feel like saying, "Sure, go on rolling your eyes. You might just find a brain back there"?
4. Don't you ever feel like saying, "Remember when I asked you for your opinion? Yeah. Me, neither"?
5. Don't you ever feel like saying, "I was hoping for a battle of wits, but you appear to be unarmed"?

Action plan

Improving?

1. Ever realize that improvement begins with "I"?
2. Do you think well enough of yourself to work harder, smarter, for greater advancement?
3. Want to improve? It's ALL in your head — stop letting yourself talk to you and instead begin talking to yourself
4. Think your critics are blocking your improvement? Don't believe everything you think. They actually promote and strengthen you! Thank them and smile.
5. Trying to improve but just keep complaining that you can'T? First, get rid of the "T" and second remember that when you complain, you remain. Poor mouth and poor life.

Action plan

_____
_____
_____
_____
_____

Gossip?

1. People will always talk about you…enjoy it by giving them something to talk about.
2. Still talking about it? Then you still care about it.
3. Want people to listen for hours? Talk to them about…themselves.
4. Do you live your life, or do you just talk about living your life?
5. Ever notice how few people can think and talk at the same time?

Action plan

_____

_____

_____

_____

_____

Wasting time?

1. Wasting time is worse than wasting money. Be careful who who spend your time with.
2. Ever notice that it's a complete waste of time trying to convince someone who's made up his/her mind when they ask you to try to convince them otherwise?
3. Wasting time on regrets keeps you from moving forward.
4. If they drag you down, why waste time with them?
5. Being nervous, worrying, fretting—a complete waste of time.

Action plan

_____
_____
_____
_____
_____

Scared?

1. Ever start anything without feeling a bit scared? That'd be a bit unusual.
2. Know what you want but feeling too scared to go after it? Don't believe everything you think.
3. Fear is grounded in negative thoughts you are using to talk you out of your dream. Stop letting yourself talk to you and begin talking to yourself.
4. Think you can be courageous without first feeling fear? Nope. Fear propels you if you know how to use it right.
5. So what's the lesson? Stop frightening yourself about anyone or anything. You hurt yourself more than what you think is so frightening.

Action plan

_____

_____

_____

_____

_____

Choosing correctly?

1. Looking for good food for your soul? Try simplicity.
2. Here's a simple rule to follow: what you have is always enough. Accomplish more, sure but not because you don't have enough. Because you enjoy accomplishing.
3. Ever consider that what you really need is…less? Try it. It'll add greatness to your life, and you'll have more.
4. Do you choose money over time and stuff over people? Whoops! You've got that wrong, don't you?
5. Why complicate things? Don't you really enjoy the simpler path? Simple is key to beauty and happiness.

Action plan

_____
_____
_____
_____
_____

Take care of yourself

1. Taking care of yourself is the best unselfish selfish necessary thing you can do for yourself
2. Are you a priority of yours?
3. So, really, c'mon, I the end whose feelings are more important than your own?
4. Want to be a better version of yourself? Then begin by taking care of yourself, your thoughts, your nutrition and your movement. Is there anything more important?
5. Take care of yourself for her and she'll take care of herself for you. It'll lead to taking care of each other, for each other. That's not selfish, it's just the opposite.

Action plan

_____

_____

_____

_____

_____

Health?

1. Let's be honest-health care is really illness care. That's why the wellness & prevention market will continue to expand.
2. Just because you are not sick doesn't mean you are well.
3. Mind-body-spirit are inseparable. Your optimal wellness depends on nourishing each of these, as one.
4. Health is about your body. Wellness is about your life.
5. Your wellness will grow when you rest, relax, revive and rejuvenate. That's renewal.

Action plan

_____

_____

_____

_____

_____

Gratitude

1. Ever notice how thankful people are happy? And here you thought it was the other way around. Try it today and see for yourself. Say "Thank You."
2. Waiting for something to be thankful for? Uh, oh. You just missed this moment. Be thankful for every moment in your life. Like this one. Oops, almost missed another. Say "Thank You."
3. Be thankful for all you have — before you ask for anything more. Asking for it and not getting it? Maybe His answer is wiser than you may think. Say "Thank You."
4. "C"mon Michael…how can I be thankful for this setback I'm facing?" Because with the right perspective, outlook and change of thinking, you'd see it as setting you up for your next victory. Say "Thank You."
5. The varsity players on Team Thankfulness say "Thank You" that thorns have roses. Say "Thank You."

Action plan

_____

_____

_____

_____

_____

Family

1. Know anything more "everything" than family?
2. Wherever you grow and go, the roots of our family insure we stay as one.
3. Forget the "mess" your kids are making…it's memories they are really making.
4. Family is a verb and a commitment, not just a feeling.
5. The real wealth of a person comes when one has something that money can't buy….have a family? You're wealthy.

Action plan

_____
_____
_____
_____
_____

Accept all of you

1. Lacking self-confidence? Oops...you've just defeated yourself once again.
2. Try feeding your self-confidence and starving your self-created fears.
3. Give yourself a large dose of WAM everyday. What's that, you ask? Tell yourself you are Wonderful, Amazing, and a Masterpiece.
4. Immediately, like right now—ok, again, NOW—no longer hear or accept anyone else's definition of your life. You define yourself. Now!
5. The next time you see someone staring or glaring at you, tell yourself s/he is taking notes...on how to be so awesome! Poof!

Action plan

_____

_____

_____

_____

_____

Don't blame them

1. Those people treat you meanly because of who THEY are, not because of who YOU are. Drop them.
2. Those people who have negative things to say about you are speaking about something that's none of your business. What they think or say about you is their business. Drop them.
3. Those people treating you badly are pathetic vagrants looking for a rent-free home in your mind and heart. Evict them. Yes, drop them.
4. Those people who talk badly about you behind your back, they wan't to infect your success, your life and your happiness. Why empower them to do so? Drop them.
5. Those people who want you to go down foolishly believe because of the degradation they feel in their own lives, that life is a see-saw and they can only go up if they push you down. Drop them.

Action plan

_____
_____
_____
_____
_____

Tranquility

1. Looking for tranquility? You won't find it while trying to conceal anything.
2. Looking for tranquility? It takes authentic resilience, healthy positive outlook and "inlook," generosity of spirit and slow awareness.
3. Looking for tranquility? Guess you are looking for the ultimate elixir, the ultimate mind medicine, the ultimate salve for anxiety, depression and anger.
4. Looking for tranquility? It's all - all - in your head. Can't find it there? Don't waste any effort at all looking elsewhere.
5. Looking for tranquility? The link is entirely what you think. It's an inside, not an outside, job.

Action plan

_____

_____

_____

_____

_____

Don't go around...

1. Hey there, yes you! Don't go around thinking your mistakes are any better than anyone else's. We all make them.
2. Hey there, yes you! Don't go around thinking your mistakes define you. They strengthen you.
3. Hey there, yes you! Don't go around turning your little rivers of mistakes into large oceans of life sentences.
4. Hey there, yes you! Don't go around thinking that one mistake ruins everything. It's the way you think that ruins everything.
5. Hey there, yes you! Don't go around thinking there's no such thing as erasers. Just focus on needing them less.

Action plan

_____

_____

_____

_____

_____

Things get better

1. Things get better...it doesn't rain and stay dark forever does it? Ever see a storm not run out of rain?
2. Things get better...you'll surely look back and realize that what looked like opposition actually made your life better.
3. Things get better...how do you know that the "no" answer you're focusing on really isn't a "yes" answer in disguise? Be patient.
4. Things get better...but it all depends on you thinking better first.
5. Things get better...they simply always do. The Potter isn't finished spinning you on His wheel, so why think He is?

Action plan

_____
_____
_____
_____
_____

The neighborhood of your mind

1. Is your mind a safe neighborhood where you can go alone at night, or is it filled with danger? It's fully your choice.
2. Want to improve the neighborhood in your mind? Invite in the spirit of gratitude, for everything, no matter what.
3. Trying to improve your mind but can't see the good in everything? Instead of just going through a situation, see how you are growing through it. Improving already!
4. The only cause of unhappiness is ALL in your head. You completely talk it all into yourself. What the heck are you doing that for?
5. Sure it may easier to condemn than to think positively. But the harm you do to yourself - not others - is far greater when you condemn.

Action plan

_____
_____
_____
_____
_____

Your inner compass

1. Do you trust your own inner compass? Follow it and don't get confused by anyone else's.
2. Don't you find that you often know more than you thought you did? That's your inner compass…trust it.
3. When you've got your own back, you never have to apologize for trusting your own intuition. When you do, take control.
4. If you are a glutton for serenity, then trust completely in yourself, your instincts, your abilities and your resilience. That trust can only come from a well-ordered mind and that mind will lead to tranquility.
5. When you truly trust yourself, you know that regardless of what happens in life, every rejection is nothing more than a welcome redirection.

Action plan

_____

_____

_____

_____

_____

Tough time?

1. Going through a tough time? Be sure you aren't asking, "Why me?" Instead challenge, "Try me!"
2. Going through a tough time? What's it got to do with how you choose to make yourself feel?
3. Going through a tough time? Maybe that's the problem. You are going through it, not growing through it.
4. Going through a tough time? God doesn't promise a smooth flight, just a safe landing.
5. Going through a tough time? The only way to reach a peak is with a good base camp. Choose your friends wisely.

Action plan

_____

_____

_____

_____

_____

Facebooking?

1. Are you in Facebook because you're bored or are you bored because you're on Facebook?
2. Why do people who hate Facebook post on Facebook that they hate Facebook?
3. Here's a flash fact: actions speak louder than "like" buttons. Remember real life actions?
4. You know when someone with no mutual friends adds you to Facebook and you have that "Who are you and how did you find me" feeling?
5. Ever realize that having five thousand friends on Facebook is just like being wealthy in Monopoly?

Action plan

_____
_____
_____
_____
_____

Self-Control

1. Do you ever let the things you cannot control, control the things you can control? Not real smart is it?
2. Do you realize that what you have the power to do, let's say eat, exercise, spend, means that you also have the power to NOT to do those things? It's called self-control.
3. Do you let your beliefs rule you, or do you rule your beliefs? What's the decision here? Control your mind.
4. Do you think your passions get you in trouble? Nope. Never. It's your lack of control that does it. It's your mind, not your passion, that you need to control first.
5. Do you believe that it's the mountain you have to conquer? Nope. Never. It's yourself you ultimately conquer, your thoughts, your beliefs, your attitudes. The link to self-control, yep, is what you think.

Action plan

_____

_____

_____

_____

_____

Ready to change?

1. Want to change something in your life? You can't...until and unless you change something going on inside of you first. Try your thinking before anything else.
2. The good news is, it only takes one person to change your life. Yep, the bad news for some is, that one person is...you.
3. The funny thing about change is that nothing changes if nothing changes. And by the way, you may need to give that change some time to change.
4. Ready to change? Here's the secret: don't waste time fighting the old, but instead, build the new.
5. Be thankful for all of those "difficult people" (ok, assholes), you've invited into your life. Seriously. Be thankful for them. They've shown you exactly what you do not want to be.

Action plan

_____

_____

_____

_____

_____

Why waste time?

1. Why waste time on something that doesn't add to your life—if it's not adding, it doesn't belong in your life.
2. Why waste your time on people who don't value your time?
3. Why waste time on explanations? People only hear and believe what they want to.
4. Why waste time on trying to show people qualities that you don't really have?
5. Why waste time making life shorter than it already is by wasting time on regretting anything? It's a fool's waste of time to regret anything.

Action plan

_____

_____

_____

_____

_____

What are you believing?

1. Great thinkers know HOW to think. Average thinkers know WHAT to think.
2. Please, please, please, for your own physical and emotional, even spiritual wellbeing, do not, I repeat, do not believe everything you think.
3. Have you matured enough yet to see that what was "freethinking" at one point in your life is now simply common sense?
4. If you are in a group of people and everyone's thinking alike, including you, then you aren't thinking.
5. If all you are thinking about are your problems, it's time, immediately, to begin thinking about solutions.

Action plan

_____
_____
_____
_____
_____

Better days...

1. Wake up this morning? Alive? Then there's hope for a better day. Always.
2. Trying to build a better life, without becoming a better person first? It won't happen. The formula is first you, then your life.
3. Want better days ahead? Toss the complexities you're adding and keep it simple. It's already a better day, isn't it?
4. Seeking better days and a better life ahead? Complain less and praise more, show more gratitude, give more than you want, have more hope than fear, build strong enjoyable relationships including with yourself, run your own race and don't compare yourself to others.
5. Sometimes having a better life takes nothing more than seeing the one you have as already better.

Action plan

_____
_____
_____
_____
_____

Feeling better already

1. What I've learned is that living a good life depends on assuming as little as possible, needing as little as possible, doing as much as possible, smiling and laughing as much as possible, and realizing how many blessings we have.
2. If you have a better goal than serving and helping others, please let me know. For me, that's the main meaning of living.
3. Forget milestones and focus on moments instead.
4. The only limit in your life is yourself - what you think - so stop complaining and blaming and start thinking victory, advancement, upward and onward.
5. Oh, so you think you'd be happier if you were richer? Dummy. Count those things you have that money can't buy. Feel better? Good.

Action plan

_____

_____

_____

_____

_____

Peace of mind

1. Really want peace of mind? Stop trying to change everyone else.
2. Really want peace of mind? Start by increasing the time you spend on self-care and decreasing the time you spend <u>NOT</u> being active. It's time.
3. Really want peace of mind? Build your optimism. The more you talk about what can go wrong, the less peace you'll have.
4. Really want peace of mind? Remember that others have the right to their nasty, negative opinion. You have the right to ignore it.
5. Really want peace of mind? Believe that no matter what happens, everything will shift in your favor. What if you are wrong? But whhat if you are right???

Action plan

_____

_____

_____

_____

_____

Accomplish anything lately?

1. Stop living for compliments and start living for accomplishments
2. Complaining about obstacles in your way? Naive. They are the building blocks of great accomplishments.
3. Doesn't iron sharpen iron? Want to accomplish something? Then surround yourself with people who have already where you want to be and do what you want to do.
4. That nonsense story you are telling yourself is the only thing between you and what you want to accomplish.
5. When you feel at your weakest is when you need to change your thinking in order to feel your strongest — how else will you accomplish anything?

Action plan

_____
_____
_____
_____
_____

Good advice for today

1. Being amazing doesn't just happen. But it always can. Never too soon - never too late. And it's all entirely up to you and that story you tell yourself.
2. Want to be someone of accomplishment? It'll never happen sitting back being jealous of others. It'll only happen if you make it happen, for yourself.
3. You know those people who don't like you? It really has nothing to do with you. Surely don't let them control your mind or your feelings. That's your choice.
4. Why hang around those who drag you down? Fill your life with people who life you higher, and who you lift.
5. Now get this: there's no such thing as perfect people…those perfect people are fake. And those "real" people? They aren't perfect.

Action plan

_____
_____
_____
_____
_____

Negative thinking pill

1. Do you seriously think there's anything "wrong" or "ill" with you that retraining and reprogramming your thoughts won't improve?
2. With thousands of thoughts you carry daily, what good are you getting from magnifying only the negative ones?
3. Don't waste those painful thoughts…they will promote you, not stop you…when you see clearly.
4. The only — only —thing that can ever make you unhappy or "insane" are your own thoughts. Pretty, pretty pretty powerful, don't you agree? So why give that power to anything or anyone else? You seriously think your critics limit you?
5. It's ALL in your head…when you let your dream fully enter into your mindset, you'll achieve your goals. Until then, you're blocking your advancement and believing it's "it" or "them" who stop you.

Action plan

_____
_____
_____
_____
_____

Leadership...good leadership

1. Good leaders? They don't - ever - condemn, criticize or judge others.
2. Good leaders? They encourage others with a gentle tongue.
3. Good leaders? Their purpose in life aligns with their actions, they are focused on their purpose.
4. Good leaders? They see the positive in others, in themselves, in their organizations through a lens of accurate self-awareness, vulnerability, ambition that includes the greater good and curiosity.
5. Good leaders? They choose happiness and never let things steal their joy.

Action plan

_____

_____

_____

_____

_____

Work ethic

1. When it comes to success in business, work ethic stands at the top of the list — takes a million dollar work ethic to make that.
2. But next, comes ambition for the greater good (not just yourself), being curious, humble, vulnerable and aspiring for success according to your vision.
3. Work ethic means doing what is right, not easy; giving a damn; doing what you say you're going to do and when you say you're going to do it; focus; take the initiative.
4. Work ethic levels the playing field when it comes to advantages in life.
5. Always be the hardest worker in the room — there's no such thing as the smartest person in the room, and even if there was, hard work trumps big lazy brains.

Action plan

_____

_____

_____

_____

_____

"What, Me Worry?"

1. Heard the saying, "Don't worry yourself sick?" Ever take that seriously? Worrying affects your physical & mental wellbeing and steals your time. "What, Me Worry?"
2. Are you a fool, worrying about things you can't control or influence? After all only fools pay debts they don't owe. And they're liable to suffer adversities twice over. "What, Me Worry?"
3. Do you do what you can do, or do you worry about what you can't do? If you want to improve your overall health, you'll put an end to that immobilizing worrying mindset right now. "What, Me Worry?"
4. Get busy - it may help you stop being busy...worrying. You aren't worrying yourself that you won't be able to stop worrying, are you? "What, Me Worry?"
5. Have you ever prayed for the worst possible outcome to happen? That's what worrying is — feeding thoughts that'll lead to what you don't want to happen.

Action plan

_____
_____
_____
_____
_____

Your intuition...trust it

1. You know how you pick up other people's vibes? That's a sacred gift that gives outlook and insight called your intuitive mind. Pay attention.
2. When you carefully follow your intuitive sense, you'll experience more innovative power, energy and a flow you've rarely felt.
3. Ever notice how your heart seems to be dialed into something that your mind just doesn't get? Enjoy it. It'll protect you until the end of your days. That's your intuitive speaking.
4. How do I know it? My intuition spoke to me. I listened and never apologize for doing so. My intuitive mind always points my thinking mind where to turn next. Power!
5. Rarely if ever, look outside of yourself for answers, truth or direction. It's rarely, if ever there. If you do, you'll weaken your intuitive perception of reality.

Action plan

_____
_____
_____
_____
_____

Today...have a great one

1. Isn't today a good day to have a great day?
2. Today, in order to have a great day...simply be better than you ever thought you could be.
3. The place to start having a great day is in your attitude, your thoughts —start by believing that something wonderful is about to happen. That small positive thought can chart the whole course.
4. So you want to have a great day today and then you go and let idiots ruin it? Don't give the idiots even a minute of your 24 hours. (Sorry idiots)
5. There's a proverb that says that a "misty morning doesn't signify a cloudy day." So why do you continually feed the belief that it does? Won't help you have a great day.

Action plan

_____
_____
_____
_____
_____

Getting older? So what?

1. Notice that the older you become the more you hear what people don't say?
2. Getting older? So what? The older the fiddle, the sweeter the tune.
3. Don't think of it as getting older…think of it as getting riper :-)
4. Isn't it wonderful that it takes so long to get older?
5. Some get older and wiser…some get older and wider. Which are you choosing?

Action plan

_____

_____

_____

_____

_____

Laughter

1. Isn't life better when you are laughing? So, why aren't you? Don't you see the humor right in front of you?
2. One of the best tools ever packed into a survival kit is a sense of humor...and a smile to go along with it.
3. Without laughter, today could just be a big waste. C'mon, it's the best, and least expensive, medicine...OD on it once in awhile.
4. No sense of humor? In that case, you could have no sense at all.
5. Looking for a tranquilizer with no bad side effects? It's called laughter. Take a dose several times a day and watch how more relaxed you fell.

Action plan

_____

_____

_____

_____

_____

EWOP Everything works out perfectly

1. C'mon, after all of this time you know full well that eventually all of the pieces fall into place and everything happens for a good reason.
2. Until it all works out well, laugh at the confusion and live in the present moment….that'd be now…now…now.
3. But Michael what do you mean it all works out in the end? It hasn't worked out! Then, my friend, it's not the end.
4. What are you worrying about? It is never as bad as you sometimes think it is. Keep a happy spirit and you'll smile when you see that it did all work out.
5. Instead of being fearful that it won't work out, be curious about how it will.

Action plan

_____
_____
_____
_____
_____

Positivity will get you there

1. Fill your mind with positivity and your life begins to change for the better. Easier said than done, true. But do it anyway.
2. Do you believe in the person you want to become?
3. Ever try to beat someone who just never gives up? Why isn't that you?
4. Don't you love doing what others say you can't do? Keep in mind that of course you can.
5. It's all mental - fitness and your ass - these won't go where your mind doesn't push them.

Action plan

_____

_____

_____

_____

_____

Crush your erroneous beliefs

1. If you (erroneously) believe that only sunshine brings happiness, or (irrationally) tell yourself you just need to wait for the storm to pass, you've never learned to dance in the rain.
2. Don't ever put up your umbrella before it starts to rain...and when it does start, stay calm, walk slowly in the rain and enjoy getting wet.
3. Whatever you do, don't allow anyone, every, to pee on your leg and try to convince you it's raining outside. Never. Ever. Allow. That.
4. You can focus on the rain or you can envision the sun shining above the clouds.
5. Is there anything better than being inside on a rainy day with someone you love, enjoying a good book, listening to peaceful music, savoring a cup of wonderful tea, and just being entranced watching the rain land on your window?

Action plan

_____
_____
_____
_____
_____

Lighten it up

1. Lighten up — life isn't nearly as serious as your mind makes it out to be.
2. Do you know anything that can stand up to laughter? It's been said that humor is our greatest blessing—lighten it up.
3. You find it offensive and I find it funny. That's why I'm happier than you. I'm not being immature — I'm just having fun. Try it and lighten it up.
4. Some say don't quit your day job. I say don't quit your day dream—it'll lighten you up.
5. Be someone who lightens up a room when they walk in, others when they walk out. Which are you?

Action plan

_____

_____

_____

_____

_____

Nothing to prove

1. Let's begin with this: you are enough. You have nothing to prove to anyone. Anyone.
2. Why look for, or rely on, the encouragement of others? It's often inauthentic, insufficient or not given when you need it.
3. Don't you think that a word of encouragement after a misstep is worth more than an hour of praise after a success?
4. Hope, praise and encouragement — open the door to success and powerful people building.
5. Never give up. Ever. That struggle you are dealing with today is just building your strength for tomorrow. How's that for encouragement to keep going?

Action plan

_____

_____

_____

_____

_____

Making peace

1. Every morning is a rebirth—be aware of that and watch what good the new day can bring.
2. Every problem known to mankind begins in the mind. It's all an illusion. Good or bad is just the way you see it.
3. Make peace with imperfection in your life—it means letting go of shit in order to embrace a fresh start.
4. Embrace vulnerability, and the fact that things come and go... that's self-compassion.
5. If you are not fully in the present, not fully aware of yourself, you'll miss a big part of your life. It's here, now, in front of you, not there, then, later.

Action plan

_____

_____

_____

_____

_____

Accepting you

1. What lifts you up or tears you down is ONLY what you tell yourself.
2. Stop looking for the 3 steps, 5 steps or magical 7 steps to success. There's only 1. Believe in yourself.
3. Mistake? So what? Keep on believing in yourself and move on.
4. When you see evil as the chair for good, you'll understand how you can continue believing in yourself, no matter what.
5. Instead of worrying about what others think about you, be sure your thoughts about you are loving and accepting.

Action plan

_____

_____

_____

_____

_____

Transform

1. When you go beyond your form, you are transitioning.
2. Every obstacle you face is nothing more than a chance to transition. Will you see it that way or as a stop sign with no "go" sign in sight?
3. Thinking of acting the way you usually do? That'll only keep you locked in your past. Transformational thinking is what's needed.
4. Transformational reform requires that you stop betting against yourself. In other words, knock off the worry.
5. Transformation of yourself, or your entire world, requires you change your words.

Action plan

_____

_____

_____

_____

_____

Family

1. Is there anything more important than family?
2. Want to learn about someone's character? Look at how s/he treats his/her family.
3. Roots, and wings...the best gifts to give your children
4. Blood makes a family? No. Love makes a family.
5. Home, like Rome, wasn't built in a day. It takes a lifetime.

Action plan

_____

_____

_____

_____

_____

S L O W down

1. Notice how, when you s l o w it down, you feel the world around you more deeply?
2. Here's an idea —s l o w down your pursuit of happiness, and just be happy.
3. Increasing the speed of life may shorten your life.
4. Want to feel better? Find a spot to s t o p and be quiet (in our head, too).
5. Want to know the best way to speed up? S L O W down.

Action plan

_____

_____

_____

_____

_____

Trust your inner voice

1. Your intuitive knowledge resides in your soul. Honor it, feed it, and recognize it as the gift it is.
2. Confused? Bewildered? Mixed-up? Follow your intuitive voice. You can trust it.
3. "My intuition tells me…" Think or say that often? Hmm, perhaps it'd be a good idea to start having the courage to do so.
4. Don't complicate your intuitive voice — it's just a higher level of understanding, and one that can save you from disaster.
5. Prepare your mind for your essence, your intuitive voice, to flourish — it grows right there, in your higher self.

Action plan

_____

_____

_____

_____

_____

Be independent

1. Never, ever, be afraid to walk this world independent, original and alone. Why? Behind every successful person is…her/himself.
2. If there's one thing to be independent of, it's the opinion of others.
3. It's been said that an independent and free media is essential to ensure democracy. Boy is democracy in trouble if that's true. Independent????
4. The relationship between happiness and external conditions epitomizes the meaning of independence. Happiness is being independent. And don't you forget that.
5. Do the right thing on your own…that's independence. Doing your own thing? Ehhh, not so sure that's independence.

Action plan

_____

_____

_____

_____

_____

Talking to yourself

1. Talk to yourself and finish this: positively "At least I"m_____."
2. Talk to yourself and finish this positively: "Who'd have thought I _____."
3. Talk to yourself and finish this positively: "I am_____."
4. Talk to yourself like you would talk with someone you love - otherwise you are giving up on self-esteem.
5. Talk to yourself and say, "I can' imagine anything better than being me."

Action plan

_____

_____

_____

_____

_____

Treating something you can prevent?

1. Why treat what you can prevent? Oh you own a treatment company? Oh then I get it.
2. Want to reduce health (illness) care demand and costs? Prevent more diseases.
3. I've long said the prevention market will overtake the treatment market. Agree?
4. The best medical care is to inform people how not to need them.
5. Stress treatment? Nonsense. Why treat what you can prevent? Why create stress and then need to treat it?

Action plan

_____
_____
_____
_____
_____

Mirror, mirror on the wall

1. I'd love to see the look that some would have if they saw their character instead of their faces when they look in the mirror.
2. "Mirror mirror on the wall, who is the most self-righteous of them all?"
3. Sometimes the most authentic people are covered in tattoos while the most negatively judgmental gossipers are found leading religious institutions.
4. You can be an asshole without being self-righteous, but you can't be self-righteous without being an asshole.
5. Moral indignation makes nobody a saint.

Action plan

_____

_____

_____

_____

_____

Be kind

1. Who really needs a reason to be kind to anyone?
2. Kindness is the best religion to follow.
3. Looking for a really special gift? Give kindness - not only will it lift someone else, but it'll lift you too.
4. More & less. Guess which? Kindness, hurry, laughter and worry.
5. When you give with authentic kindness, you don't count the cost.

Action plan

_____
_____
_____
_____
_____

Being successful

1. Real success is not tied to a time limit. You'll achieve it when you achieve it.
2. Bring your passion and your career into alignment and you'll see the success you imagined.
3. Success begins in your mind. Be sure you are not talking yourself out of the success you want.
4. Success is truly yours for the taking. Take it.
5. Sometimes the best career moves are not the ones you planned for, but were the ones you were open to.

Action plan

_____
_____
_____
_____
_____

Chill out

1. Life is really so much easier when you just chill out.
2. What's chilling? Doing nothing and not being bored.
3. Keep calm and trust. That'll help you chill.
4. Telling someone who's upset to chill out, won't work.
5. No time to chill? That means only one thing. You definitely need to chill. Now.

Action plan

_____
_____
_____
_____
_____

Perfect imperfection

1. Light bulb burned out the other day. Guess what? Didn't buy a new home. Just bought a new light bulb. It's not ever all or nothing It's imperfect.
2. I gave up perfection long ago. Excellence, grace, progress and being real are different. Those I"ll never give up.
3. What's with people? Fearing rejection, wanting attention, craving affection and dreaming of perfection.
4. Instead of "perfect" beauty, how about confidence, character and charisma? Aren't they achievable beauty?
5. Notice how to spell "imperfect"? That'd be "I'm perfect." Hmmm, could it be that perfect is really being imperfect?

Action plan

Blaming?

1. Stop blaming others because you are unhappy. It's your job to make yourself happy even if others make themselves unhappy as a result.
2. Do nice things for others today, and everyday. Don't you feel better?
3. Of course you are fallible. That's the definition of normal. Ohhhh, you thought you were supposed to be perfect? How foolish.
4. It isn't always about you. Stop personalizing so much. Maybe the other person is just not in a good mood or is - imagine this - focused on their own trouble and not on you.
5. So you tripped, failed, made a mistake. So what? No successful person that I've ever coached, has never stumbled. Win or learn. Never lose.

Action plan

_____
_____
_____
_____
_____

Keys to your happiness

1. Look beyond imperfection
2. Pursue, fearlessly, what lights you up
3. Talking with a fool? Shhh. Smile to yourself. Walk away happy
4. You are your standard, your own sunshine. That'll lead to your happiness
5. The key to your happiness is in your own pocket...it's a word, "regardless,"and when used properly frees you to smile

Action plan

_____

_____

_____

_____

_____

Let go

1. Own your self-worth...never give another's opinion of you the ability to determine anything about you
2. Pick your battles wisely, forgive those who truly harm you in order to free yourself to advance, yet don't give them a second chance to do it again
3. Where are you focused? On the past? On your problems? Don't let your past errors be your present reality. Your misfortunes can be your fortunes when you focus on learning and solutions
4. Let go...of negativity, of negative people, of grudges, of thoughts that create stress
5. Learn to say "no" comfortably with no excuses, "I don't want to" sounds more honest than "Oh I'm sorry I can't"

Action plan

_____

_____

_____

_____

_____

Living fully

1. Live life fully, not catering to your inner doubt, ridding your path of toxic people as soon as you recognize it
2. Care genuinely about yourself, others, the quality of whatever you do & your deeply felt purpose
3. Believe in your ability to succeed, seeing setbacks as setups to come back
4. Always remember to give credit - humility will help you recognize that your success is a shared adventure
5. Be certain your tough-mindedness builds skills in perseverance. Giving up is never a viable option. Fearful? Do it anyway

Action plan

_____

_____

_____

_____

_____

ABOUT THE AUTHOR

Michael R. Mantell is a best-selling author of three earlier books, an international keynote speaker in behavior science of leadership, fitness and life transformation, and is a highly sought after positive people builder. He has served as an Advisor to many of the country's leading gyms and fitness equipment manufacturers, digital tech and financial organizations, as well as to government leaders and institutions.

Dr. Mantell earned his Ph.D. at the University of Pennsylvania and his M.S. degree at Hahnemann Medical College, where he wrote his thesis on the psychological aspects of obesity. After serving as Chief Psychologist for Children's Hospital in San Diego, he created and led the program of Psychological Services for the San Diego Police Department. He has been an Assistant Clinical Professor in the Department of Psychiatry at UCSD Medical School. He went on to become the Senior Fitness Consultant for Behavior Sciences for the American Council on Exercise and is currently the Director of Transformational Behavior Coaching for the Premier Fitness Camp, Omni La Costa Resort and Spa. Dr. Mantell serves on the Science Advisory Board of the International Council on Active Aging.

As a member of SAG/AFTRA since 1981, Dr. Mantell has appeared regularly on "Good Morning America," CBS-TV, ABC-TV, Fox News and the CW in San Diego. He's appeared on Oprah, Larry King Live, "The Today Show," hosted two highly popular Podcasts, and been featured in many of the nation's top health-fitness magazines, national and international newspapers and general interest publications. Dr. Mantell is a Wexner Foundation Fellow and is listed in greatist.com's "*The 100 Most Influential People in Health and Fitness.*"

He coaches business leaders, elite amateur and professional athletes, individuals, couples, families and A-list celebrities who are seeking optimal levels of health, personal and professional success, improved performance and genuine life satisfaction.

Previous books:

Don't Sweat the Small Stuff PS: It's All Small Stuff, 1988

Ticking Bombs: Defusing Violence in the Workplace, 1996

The 25th Anniversary Edition of Don't Sweat the Small Stuff PS It's All Small Stuff, 2014

Connect with Dr. Mantell

Ready to transform your life, the life of your company and your employees? Want to feel more motivated, inspired and fully prepared to achieve your dreams?

It's time to book an entertaining, powerfully transformative speaking engagement with Dr. Mantell, live or as a webinar, and take the next step for yourself and your employees to living better, fuller and more successfully.

He brings organization his decades of experience in the psychology of success, with his highly sought after personal and warm style. Dr. Mantell never fails helping his world-wide audiences crush their self-created obstacles and turning their personal stumbling blocks into professional stepping stones.

Want more of Dr. Mantell's practical tools? Subscribe to his newsletter where you'll receive his "Daily 5" and more.

Would you like even more personalized transformational coaching directly from Dr. Mantell? He speaks with folks from every walk of life throughout the world helping them change their thinking to insure living better, healthier and with stress-free peace of mind.

Contact Dr. Mantell for further information on speaking engagements and newsletter subscription on Linkedin at Michael Mantell, Ph.D. or on Twitter at @DrSanDiego and @FitnessPsych .

Made in the USA
Middletown, DE
06 December 2018